Nonprofit Mergers

The Power of Successful Partnerships

Aspen's Nonprofit Management Series

Extraordinary Board Leadership:
The Seven Keys to High-Impact Governance

Doug Eadie

Nonprofit Mergers: The Power of Successful Partnerships

Dan H. McCormick

Aspen's Nonprofit Management Series

Nonprofit Mergers

The Power of Successful Partnerships

Dan H. McCormick, MM
President and Chief Executive Officer
McCormick Group, EFC
Williamston, Michigan

AN ASPEN PUBLICATION®
Aspen Publishers, Inc.
Gaithersburg, Maryland
2001

Library of Congress Cataloging-in-Publication Data
McCormick, Dan H.
Nonprofit mergers: the power of successful partnerships/Dan H. McCormick.
p. cm. — (Aspen's nonprofit management series)
Includes bibliographical references and index.
ISBN 0-8342-1832-1 (alk. paper)
1. Nonprofit organizations. 2. Consolidation and merger of corporations.
3. Strategic alliances (Business) I. Title. II. Series
HD2769.15.M334 2001
658.1'6--dc21   00-062063

Orders: (800) 638-8437
Customer Service: (800) 234-1660

Editorial Services: Irene Vartanoff
Library of Congress Catalog Card Number: 00-062063
ISBN: 0-8342-1832-1

Printed in the United States of America

1 2 3 4 5

Table of Contents

Foreword

THE POWER OF SUCCESSFUL PARTNERSHIPS

THE RESTRUCTURING OF ANY LARGE ORGANIZATION can be a monumental endeavor. In any such undertaking, there are innumerable obstacles to overcome—some structural, others cultural. Mergers, in particular, present their own unique challenges, often centering around the commingling of corporate cultures and the sense of loss and displacement that staff and volunteers may feel. Even when corporations or nonprofits are at the breaking point and there would seem to be no other reasonable alternatives to restructuring, apathy, inertia, and hostility can combine with the inevitable logistical and operational issues to undermine success. It need not be this way.

To succeed, mergers must be carefully planned and professionally executed. The case for change must be made forcefully, and the needs and interests of all parties taken into account throughout the process. It is simply not possible to satisfy everyone, but reasonable people will be persuaded by reasonable arguments. Throughout the process, it is important to remember that the point of mergers is not to make people happy, but to advance the mission and the goals of an organization. Ultimately, this is the yardstick by which organizational change must be measured.

A well-planned and well-executed merger can advance an organization's mission and will usually accomplish much more, but unless care is taken from the outset to gain input and build consensus, there's no guarantee that the finished product will live up to its potential or that the merged entity will be better than its parts. This is especially true in the nonprofit world, where the organization's primary mission is not creating wealth for the owners and shareholders but improving the world in which we live. A corporation's bottom line is quite easy to gauge and is a compelling argument in and of itself. However, the ideals expressed in a nonprofit's mission are often much harder to measure and more open to interpretation. One person's notion of success may not be the same as another's.

For many people the concept of merger suggests both the leveraging of resources and a concomitant strengthening of the corporate infrastructure; for others it is simply a buzz word for unnecessary change—or worse, change necessitated by the past failures of management. Both can be true, and rarely is either completely wrong. This difference in perceptions is critically important for those who hope to effect significant, lasting, and ultimately productive change. Success may be predicated on the ability of managers to overcome cynicism and indifference and reinforce the positive results that can be achieved.

The American Cancer Society (originally, the American Society for the Control of Cancer) was founded in 1913 in New York City by a handful of successful professionals. Its purpose was to educate the public and the medical community about both the dangers of cancer and the possibilities offered by early diagnosis and treatment. Initially, the Society was concentrated on the east coast and led by an elite group of physicians and businessmen. The Society quickly developed a reputation as the leading source of unbiased cancer information. Many looked to these individuals for advice and guidance in the treatment and control of cancer. However, not everyone was willing to recognize its authority, in part because of the organization's localized nature, and in the years immediately following the Society's founding, independent cancer organizations began to spring up in several states throughout the country.

The Society's founders quickly recognized that such organizations were likely to disagree on issues regarding treatment and diagnosis and that their conflicting messages could lead to fear and confusion among the public. At a meeting of the Society's Executive Committee in 1914, Dr. James Reynolds warned that "local organizations for the control of cancer are now springing up all over the country. The institution of a multiplicity of independent and often conflicting organizations is always a misfortune to the purpose for which they are organized." Dr. Reynolds proposed creating organizations that would be within the Society's national organizational structure and dedicated to its lifesaving mission.

In order to address these concerns and extend its presence into the rest of the country, the Society began to form state chapters in 1916. The strategy proved to be successful, and by 1922, the Society had established a foothold in 48 states, 10 Canadian cities, and several U.S. territories. While the Canadian chapters eventually broke away to establish the Canadian Cancer Society, the Society continued to expand its presence in the United States. In the mid-1940s, the organization was renamed as the American Cancer Society. It restructured its regional offices, replacing its chapter structure with independently chartered divisions. After this reorganization was complete, the new Society had a total of 59 divisions, one at the site of each chapter and several more in select regional and metropolitan areas.

By establishing divisions throughout the country, the Society was able to reach a much broader audience and thereby maintain its reputation as the leading cancer organization in the United States. There is little doubt that the organization would quickly have been lost among a sea of competing cancer organizations had the founder not had the foresight to expand the organization into all states and many cities. However, success had its drawbacks. Divisions in large states had access to far more resources than those in smaller states and regions. A California or Texas division could raise far more money for their efforts than a Delaware or Westchester Division, and although the smaller divisions had fewer constituents to serve, they still had significant structural and operational costs.

For many years, smaller divisions were able to stay afloat and serve their respective regions without great difficulty, but in the late 1980s a downturn in the economy, coupled with increasing competition from other cancer organizations, began to take its toll. Donations dropped off, and while many of the Society's larger divisions were able to tighten their belts and move on, its smaller ones found themselves in serious jeopardy. As the decade wore on, these divisions fell further behind, regularly falling into concurrent spending and, in the worst cases, bringing in only enough money to open the doors and turn on the lights. Little was left for services to the public.

The Society's leadership immediately recognized they had a problem but disagreed on how to resolve it. Some urged patience, arguing that the Society's structure had served it admirably and could continue to do so well into the future if larger divisions and the national office would be willing to provide some stopgap assistance until the economy picked up. Others, recognizing that real and lasting changes taking place in the market were far more likely to impact the organization than a temporary downturn in the economy, maintained that the Society needed to seriously consider long-term structural changes.

The debate raged back and forth into the 1990s as the Society's financial health continued to deteriorate. To make matters more difficult, the Society's organizational structure spreads the authority for making decisions throughout its various entities. Each division has its own chief executive officer who reports to his or her own voluntary board of directors, and the national office has both a voluntary board of directors and a voluntary assembly of delegates. The Society has always valued and in many ways profited from the breadth and diversity of its governance bodies, but this structure also made consensus building and compromise extensive elements of the decision-making process.

Eventually, it became apparent that something had to be done. In 1996, the Society began merging some of its smaller divisions into larger regional groupings. It was a challenging process. Despite the very real and pressing need to shore up these poorly financed operations, many volunteers and staff were reluctant to abandon the existing structure. In most cases, they felt strongly that the Society would lose more than it would gain through the consolidation of its offices. They feared that valuable volunteer and staff leaders would be disenfranchised and that the Society's presence in important communities would be reduced. These were legitimate concerns. Ultimately, some volunteers and staff did find their roles diminished, and some of the Society's offices were forced to close, but by and large, the merger process has proven successful.

The Society's stewardship commitment to donors and the public is at an even higher level than before, and its goal of reassigning mid-level administrative staff to conduct lifesaving programs at the community level has been achieved. In 1996 the Society had 57 divisions. Today, it has just 17, and each is on sound financial footing. In fact, many of them are enjoying record increases in income, allowing them to devote more money than ever before to cancer control, prevention, and research. In most cases, the newly merged structures have been able to reduce the number of staff working behind the scenes in various administrative capacities and significantly increase the number of staff who are directly interacting with the public to implement cancer control programs and provide patient support services.

Despite the initial concerns of some volunteers and staff, today very few do not believe that the Society's various mergers were a success and that this success was achieved through careful planning, honest and open communication, and a commitment to mission that overrode all other concerns.

The chapters that follow raise many important issues and offer critical advice for organizations that are about to embark on the process of restructuring. Dan McCormick was an essential resource throughout the Society's merger, and his thoughtful ideas and suggestions will prove to be invaluable to other nonprofit organizations that are seeking to maximize their potential and meet the challenges of the new millennium. Mergers are never easy, but in an increasingly competitive marketplace, especially in the nonprofit sector, they can mean the difference between success and failure.

John Seffrin, PhD
Chief Executive Officer
American Cancer Society

Preface

WHEN IT WAS SUGGESTED that I write a book on mergers, my initial thought was that it would be a 30-page pamphlet describing the process, warning of the pitfalls, and presenting a "must do" checklist in the back. That was before I realized that the salient issues surrounding mergers transcend the technical and embody the very fabric of nonprofit organizations. Nonprofit organization (NPO) mergers are about mission, money, members, management, and method. More important, all those factors must be carefully considered and addressed within the context of the emotion that is the fuel that makes volunteer NPOs work.

In April of 1995, I received a call from Bill Barram, vice president of field operations, western region, of the American Cancer Society, who asked me to provide some confidential thoughts on mergers within divisions of the American Cancer Society (ACS). On a plane trip from Portland to San Francisco, CA, I wrote a short concept paper and faxed it to Bill. Thus began the journey that has led to the complete reorganization of the field structure of the ACS, and, eventually, to this book.

My early reaction when given this task was, "Why me?" Mergers are ordinarily a matter of negotiations and agreement supported by a plethora of legal documents. However, it soon occurred to me that the ACS is an organization of people, and most of those people are volunteers. Also, the volunteers associated with the ACS are immersed in a tradition of service that generates great emotional attachment. It's a moving experience to hear why many of the volunteers for the American Cancer Society have served tirelessly for 20, 30, and even more years: It's almost always because of their personal cancer story. It was clear to me that the merger of American Cancer Society divisions was not a cut-and-dried legal process; rather, it was about honor, dignity, grace, and, most of all, people.

During my experiences with the ACS, it became evident that the ACS was merging much more than its divisions—it was merging people and missions.

It is my hope that those who read this book find it helpful and appreciate its focus on the critical element of volunteers and staff—not just economics, practicality, or process—involved in any merger.

Acknowledgments

I THANK BILL BARRAM AND CLINT CLAMPITT of the American Cancer Society, my working partners in all the ACS mergers, who gave me the opportunity to gain the experiences I write about. Recognition is also extended to Don Thomas, chief operating officer of the American Cancer Society for his vision and courage in moving the ACS into its current merged posture. Thanks to John Seffrin, PhD, chief executive officer of the American Cancer Society, for his leadership in guiding the American Cancer Society into becoming the world's largest health charity and for writing the foreword to this book. I thank Elizabeth Tyrrell, partner at McAfee and Taft, of Oklahoma City, OK, for her legal help in the mergers and review of the technical information in this book. To my family, Micki, Kelly, Kim, and Shawn, thank you for your continued support of my work and efforts. My thanks also go to Sarah Nelson, Beth Vanderlip, and Vanessa Martin, my superb office support team. Also, I owe Cindy Evans, my exceptional executive assistant and team member, a debt of thanks and gratitude for providing more help and support in the mergers and on this book than I could ever repay. I also thank Susan Reardon for her diligent editing and organizational suggestions, Tracy Uber for her research and assistance early on, and Patricia Payette for research and organizational contributions. I thank the American Cancer Society and the Windstar Foundation for their contribution as early nonprofit mergers, and for the use of their names and experiences in this book. Last, I want to acknowledge the thousands of staff and volunteers of the American Cancer Society, whose commitment to eradicating this disease in our lifetime is demonstrated daily in their work, contributions, and zeal. Because of them, a percentage of the sales of this book will be contributed to the American Cancer Society.

Introduction

Increasing capacity overnight. Sounds like the stuff dreams are made of? Actually, it's the stuff that happens when organizations merge. Increased capacity to do what? Ah, that's the stuff of dreams.

—Dan McCormick, December 1998

THE FIRST TIME I was involved in a merger among nonprofit organizations was, in retrospect, a very interesting experience. It is amazing that it was ever completed successfully. It was more a negotiation than a collegial effort; it was more plunder than partnership. In fact, while the talk at the table was about mission, it was clear that the real driver was asset procurement and the opportunity for the financially strong to prey on the weak. Many of us in the room were not convinced that the merger, which was based on money not mission, would survive once the principal personalities were out of the picture or lost interest. We were right. Four years later it was dissolved. Everyone lost.

The next time I had an opportunity to participate in a merger, I used that previous experience to avoid the combative atmosphere and instead create an environment for developing a merged organization that was potentially greater than the sum of its un-merged parts. The resultant entity was formed not because one was lost but rather because both together were found to be more effective.

Why am I writing a book on nonprofit mergers when you can get a technical checklist from many competent law firms? Because it is not the contracts that make nonprofit organization (NPO) mergers work, it's the context. It's more about how it feels to the participants than how it is legally structured.

Continued mergers of NPOs are inevitable. Private foundations are re-quiring like-minded NPOs to affiliate before distributing major grants. There are simply not enough philanthropic dollars to go around to keep all of the 650,000 NPOs in America viable. And those are only a few rea-sons that mergers will continue.

The importance of this book is not that it guides you and your organi-zation through the process of merging and makes any merger smoother and easier. The important thing is recognizing how a merger can improve results on your mission virtually overnight.

Upon the moment of merger, you can increase the size of your donor list geometrically, share resources, fill or abandon unused space, get out of debt, achieve economies previously unavailable to you because of size, and realize countless other positive outcomes. And, of course, let's not for-get the financial savings. How much? In my experience with more than 40 mergers, the entities involved realized an average of 4% net savings. I call it the no-brainer 4% because it literally seems to happen just because you merge.

If you are working with a nonprofit organization that (a) cares about its mission, (b) has any competition, and (c) needs to increase fundraising, volunteer recruitment, donor base, or public visibility, you should be thinking about merger.

One question often heard when the subject of merger is broached in the nonprofit community is: "Aren't mergers more appropriate in the for-profit world than in the nonprofit sector?" If you think of mergers as a purely financial exercise, then it may not be clear how mergers can benefit a nonprofit organization. However, if you think about mergers as a strategy to increase capacity, advance mission, and ensure long-term viability, then mergers, which became the staple for-profit corporate strategy of the 1980s and 1990s, are destined to become the major nonprofit organizational tactic of the next 10 years.

Another primary reason mergers will become more prevalent in the coming years is that as nonprofits begin to merge, they will begin to put more pressure on small organizations and gradually out-compete them for volunteers, donors, media attention, advocacy, and impact on their cause. For example, the American Cancer Society (ACS), in its recent intradivisional mergers, restructured its organization by merging 57 divisions into 17, the smallest of which has a budget of more than $14 million. The smallest ACS division is larger than many nationally based nonprofit organizations. By definition, ACS divisions will have a competitive advantage because of size. As pressure on small organizations mounts, they will begin to look toward merger, joint operating agreements, strategic alliances, joint ventures, and other cooperative relationships as a means of survival.

Statistics show that nonprofit mergers are on the rise and will continue to be a part of the nonprofit landscape into the new century. Although the for-profit sector dominated the merger movement before 1994 in terms of dollar volume, a major shift occurred the following year. Although mergers between small NPOs, like the Windstar Foundation example presented in this book, still do not garner media attention, it is believed that the trend is in its infancy. Further, there appears to be a slowing of for-profit mergers, although recent for-profit mergers have been massive: Glaxo Wellcome and SmithKline Beecham, America Online and Time Warner. Recent activity among other NPOs, such as the merger between Foodchain and Second Harvest, suggests that the trend is becoming more widespread. Hospitals, major charities, nonprofit insurance groups, and others are moving toward mergers in ever-increasing numbers. For more information on trends see the report on "Strategic Restructuring" by the Chapin Hall Center for Children, in Appendix L.

We need look no further than the rise in dot-com companies to see what the future holds. Because the Internet is available to everyone, it's not just the company that succeeds, it's the business model. The rapid proliferation of dot-com ventures is based on low-cost or no-cost market entry, which comes from the alliances among idea companies, marketing companies, and technical support companies. Heretofore unrelated or joined together as service providers for fees, the model companies of 2000 are joined in the work while remaining independent, all sharing in profits.

This model will move into the nonprofit arena because it works and makes sense. NPOs will become "dot-orgs" in every respect. They will form strategic structures to support their mission and business development. And these strategic structures start with mergers. Mergers produce the capital and capacity for inventiveness. Mergers take competition through cooperation to what I call "co-operation," a nonprofit corporate structure that competes better just because of the way it is organized.

CHAPTER 1

Deciding To Merge

NONPROFIT MERGERS: A DEFINITION

PERHAPS WHEN YOU HEAR the word "merger," you think of one company consuming another, and, in your mind, merger is synonymous with takeover or acquisition. But contemporary merger among nonprofits is one that organizations view as an opportunity for growth, more effective alignment of resources, and a demonstration of stewardship. A discussion of mergers should start by throwing away the misguided, but common, assumption that merger means the death of an organization or the failure of a mission. Instead, it's important to understand how mergers "can meld missions of nonprofits, thereby allowing the combined entity to better pursue a common purpose with more stability for clients, employees, and board members alike" (La Piana, 1995, p. 24). Mergers become the rebirth of an organization rather than the death of a mission.

Before examining the merger process, it is important to clarify what the term merger means. Technically, a merger is the legal act of combining two or more separate corporate entities into one corporate entity with a single governing body. However, mergers are not always between two or more separate organizations.

Sometimes they are within organizations. Mergers between two or more separate, corporate, unrelated entities are called "intermergers." Mergers between two or more organizations that are related corporately, through charter or other affiliation, are called "intramergers." As an example, mergers between affiliates of the American Lung Association would be intramergers because, even though each entity is a separate corporation, they are chartered and granted the use of the name by the American Lung Association corporate structure.

It is important to note that mergers among corporations, even if intrarelated in some fashion, require a formal merger procedure (as outlined in Chapter 5).

So how do nonprofit and for-profit mergers differ? Most for-profit mergers are motivated by financially driven or market-driven forces. For-profit corporations are usually trying to increase shareholder value or reduce the competitive environment. Nonprofit organizations tend to favor mergers driven by mission. Typically, nonprofit mergers do not focus as much on the resultant financial bottom line, nor are they entered into just to save discretionary income. What is important in nonprofit mergers is the ability to apply greater resources toward the participating organizations' causes. The rationale behind a nonprofit merger is restructuring not to save, but to ensure that every dollar raised is responsibly applied toward the mission. That is what is commonly referred to in the nonprofit world as stewardship. Thinking of merger in this way makes it evident that the decision to merge bridges the management of mission and money.

Stephen P. Wernet and Sandra A. Jones (1992) believe the difference between for-profit and nonprofit mergers and acquisitions is based on purpose. They assert that mergers occur as a strategy for growth and expansion. "In the non-profit sector, mergers and acquisitions occur as a strategy for addressing resource scarcity and environmental uncertainty" (p. 378). In an ideal nonprofit merger environment, Wernet and Jones explain, "there is equality among the actors on the dimensions of power and resources. The concern is for synergistic gains through economies of effort and marketplace competition" (p. 370). This concern for equality is a key point—in preparation for a successful merger the parties must give up any perceptions that the strong entity absorbs the weak entity. Even if the potential merging entities vary in size and budget, the power of mergers is in the fact that "virtually every organization has strengths and weaknesses. The critical focus should be on the possible interplay of the various strengths and weaknesses—how the strengths can feed on each other and how the weaknesses can be minimized or offset." (McLaughlin, 1996, p. 6). This expanded thinking allows organizations to stay focused on issues that go beyond the financial bottom line.

The senior administration and volunteer leadership of a nonprofit entity must understand that the decision to merge, and the process by which they are merging, is based on sound business principles, even if a postmerger financial pro forma is not available. What should drive the decision to merge is the organization's ability to deliver its stated mission in light of known or potential financial reward or results. In successful nonprofit mergers, a shift in application of resources occurs, rather than the traditional cost-cutting maneuvers frequently observed in for-profit mergers. These shifts might, or might not, result in substantial savings, but should be aimed at increasing capacity to perform the mission.

This notion is the guiding principle in nonprofit merger: to affect the mission positively. Given that the mission is why nonprofit organizations (NPOs) exist, there can be no other creditable driver toward merger. One must realize that, for the most part, the fact that NPOs exist is usually because either government or the private business sector is unwilling or unable to perform the needed services or conduct the programs. If NPOs were structured as money-making entities, they would eventually attract for-profit competitors. If governments could or would provide the services of NPOs, there would be no reason for NPOs' existence. That is one reason there are fewer health-related charities in countries with socialized medicine. Further, the entire NPO, nongovernmental organization system is virtually nonexistent in the formerly socialistic countries of Eastern Europe.

These facts suggest that any financial basis for merger is not important. That is certainly not true. The expectation is that a merger still increases capacity. For an NPO to increase capacity it must produce more revenue, or change how it does its work in some statistically meaningful way. A merger does exactly that. In a merger, organizations must achieve either economic advantages or efficiency advantages. In my experience, they do both.

La Piana (1995) explains that it is unlikely that the financial position of merging organizations will immediately improve after a merger. "Well-conceived and implemented mergers can raise staff morale, better focus the organization's activities, and increase overall energy levels. A successful merger can offer relief and renewed hope for nonprofit boards, staff and donors, and most importantly, benefit clients because of the greater energy, increased funding, and better management possible with a more stable organization" (p. 4). Current examples, however, indicate that a well-planned merger can produce immediate financial results. Mergers seem to be one case in which a nonprofit organization can change the tire while driving down the road. A well-conceived merger will create expanded capacity overnight.

THE EMOTION OF MERGER

For the reasons mentioned above, it would seem that nonprofit mergers should be less frightful and stressful on a personal basis than for-profit mergers. While cutting costs and taking advantage of scale economics are important, because of NPOs' focus on mission, there is usually not a stated goal of downsizing personnel or significant reduction in services. The factors that produce fear in those caught in for-profit mergers, such as loss of job, relocation, reduced pay, and less authority and responsibility in positions, are rarely a significant, direct result of a merger in NPOs.

However, the staff and volunteers associated may not see this subtle but important distinction. Their frame of reference is family, friends, and neighbors who have been affected negatively in for-profit mergers. Their fear, concern, and actions will be guided, to a large degree, by the historical perception. Maintaining appropriate levels of understanding and expectation of the end result of merger is an important challenge. It is an error to believe that everyone will immediately perceive the advantage of a merger and sign on to ensure its success.

An example of this situation can be found in the case of the Michigan Foundation for Educational Leadership. The Foundation was formed in 1990 as a supporting entity to the Michigan Association of School Boards. Its mission is to further excellence in education in Michigan schools by helping governance-level school leaders make good decisions on behalf of the students they serve.

The Foundation has been successful. It has raised a fair amount of money and established itself as a leader by instituting and continuing to sponsor a major educational summit in the state each fall.

Over the years, the Michigan Association of School Boards (MASB) has provided financial and in-kind support to the Foundation exceeding $50,000 annually. Recently, MASB has taken the position that the Foundation should be more self-sufficient.

A new organization of 22 of the most powerful educational associations and organizations in the state approached the Foundation with a proposal to merge. The Foundation met the suggestion with significant resistance.

Even in the face of declining financial support and no direct means of attracting the funds necessary to ensure long-term viable operation, the Foundation leadership perceived a sense of loss of control and a potential shift in mission. In this case, the emotion of the issue allowed the Foundation to risk a significant reduction in capacity or even extinction rather than accept a change in the scope of its mission.

While this may seem illogical to the external observer, the fact is that mission is an emotional issue. NPO mission statements are about service and attention to causes, not like their for-profit counterparts whose mission statements talk about financial security and market leadership.

The fears evident in NPO mergers are centered among volunteers and staff in the perception of loss that one or more merging partners experience related to mission, tradition, or culture. NPOs tend to have strong relationships that form between and among volunteers, staff, supporters, and receivers of services. It is this emotional and sometimes quasi-social change in the organizations that produces the fear of what the merge will bring and a sense of loss.

Immediately, the problem of achieving volunteer and staff approval of merger becomes evident. If the leadership cannot produce a defendable financial pro forma about the anticipated financial implications of the merger, and, if strong emotional issues lead membership away from making such a drastic change, upon what do organizations build a case that will drive them toward a merger decision?

REASONS TO MERGE

"As [you begin] to articulate the reasons to merge, it is vital to begin by identifying a central compelling reason that a merger would be beneficial for your non-profit organization" (Greif, 1990, p. 35). Once you have defined this central, mission-based rationale, you'll need to consider other supporting evidence that will influence your organization's postmerger identity. An effective merger should provide the new entity with greater capacity to have a positive impact in as many of the following areas as possible:

- Greater organizational efficiency through combining positions, reducing administrative costs, and streamlining standardized operations.

- Increased effectiveness of client/constituent service through concentrating a greater percentage of staff support at the service level and using the best practices of the individual entities.

- Greater financial stability through combining the financial resources of both organizations. Debt becomes a smaller percentage of the total budget, and there may be a leveling of the impact of ebb-and-flow cycles of fund development.

- Increased market power as the constituency bases of individual organizations are joined into one entity. The flurry of activity and information flow surrounding the merger brings attention to the new organization and provides a platform to reconnect current and lapsed constituencies.

- Enhanced community image through the merger activity by stimulating media attention and demonstrating the organization's commitment to effective stewardship of funds.

- Increased power and prestige through increased size and the relative impact of the stronger voice of the newly merged entity. After a merger, the new organization's statements and public policy positions carry more political weight because of the potential impact on the enlarged constituency base.

- Reduced competitive fundraising when donor databases and funding strategies are joined under one organization.

FORCES DRIVING MERGERS

In addition to reasons to consider merger, there are also drivers that propel an organization to consider merger. These forces frequently are re-

actions to existing or expected conditions that lie outside the strategic objectives and mission-driven goals of a merger. These drivers are conditions
that seem to require merger rather than satisfy a desire to merge.

Driving forces are important considerations because they are usually
connected to one or more of the compelling reasons to merge. Most organizations, given their choice, would prefer autonomy to merger; these
drivers contribute to removing the option. These same forces also set the
stage for merger negotiations. While merger may be a conscious decision
by the leadership to increase mission or organizational capacity, it frequently is driven by one or more of the following forces: liability, viability,
or survivability.

Liability

Liability can take many forms, from financial liability to political liability. A nonprofit organization that made a decision to buy or build a
new facility and has a debt service that significantly reduces mission-
related work is at risk of allowing liability to destroy the organization. Additionally, an organization whose work and mission exposes it to potential litigation that might put it at risk may wish to consider merger.

Another liability driver could be wishing to remove negative public
image due to an employer's or director's inappropriate behavior. Sometimes liability drivers take on less obvious forms, such as potential for future litigious action from a long past action or inaction.

As an example, in 1992 the Windstar Foundation, an Aspen,
CO–based organization focusing on environmental issues and planetary
sustainability, found itself with 1,500 acres of pristine mountain valley
land that carried nearly $1 million in debt. Realizing that its primary sup-
port emanated from a few individuals and an annual symposium with a
history of netting less than anticipated, it appeared the financial liability
would drive Windstar to dissolution, then defaulting on its loans and re-

turning the land to the bank lenders. Volunteer leadership decided the land was more important than operational activities. They found and successfully merged with the National Wildlife Federation, which aligned philosophically with the Windstar Foundation, and, by giving up control of its own board of directors, gained assurance that the land would be protected. Windstar was even able to conduct some of its mission-related core activities (see Windstar Foundation—A Case History, Appendix A).

Viability

Questioned viability is a condition in which your organization may be alive, but it may not be having a positive impact on its mission. This condition is characterized by high administrative and fundraising expenditures that are not offset by incoming support dollars. If your organization has hit a plateau that lasts three or more years in the areas of volunteer and membership recruitment, fundraising efforts, and total incoming support dollars, your work may no longer be publicly viable in relationship to your mission.

Many organizations try to hang on until it becomes too late to recover from such positions. Further, some organizations suffer for many years with low productive staff leadership and dwindling volunteer participation. Most NPOs move slowly to remove the people, both staff and volunteers, that are impeding their optimal success.

An additional issue arises when antiquated business practices and processes slowly bleed the organization into a position of low viability. Most NPOs account for their funds with a process called "functional allocation." This system is effective for determining how much of someone's time is spent on one activity or another, but it rarely provides an accurate account of what a program or business practice really costs. Such inattention can result in organizations' conducting operations at a loss, slowly draining or reducing the financial capacity to a place where recovery is next to impossible. Exhibit 1–1 lists other signs of a troubled NPO.

Exhibit 1–1 Signs of a Troubled NPO

1. Stagnant amount or loss in total funds raised

2. Loss of percentage of total philanthropic market

3. Stagnant number or loss in number of volunteers

4. Mounting debt load

5. Observable excess capacity in facility or personnel

6. Gradual loss of financial reserves as they are being used for operation

7. Unusually high turnover rate of employees especially at middle and senior levels

8. Loss in the perception of value or need for the mission by constituents and the public

9. Consistent pattern of unfavorable media

10. Increased difficulty in recruitment of qualified and competent board members and volunteer leadership

Viability also is an issue for organizations whose mission is nearly complete, is no longer perceived as critical, or has fallen out of the favor of its public. These entities may find that merger is a more effective alternative than adopting a new mission and reorganizing. Entities that are merely staying afloat, but are not truly viable, should consider merger before viability becomes a question of survivability.

One example of this is the American Lung Association (ALA). The ALA has very strong name recognition. The organization is supported by numerous state and local affiliates that raise funds and, like many other charities, submit a percentage of their money to the national office. The ALA grew out of an era when tuberculosis (TB) was a major health threat in this country and worldwide. With advances in medical capacity to deal with TB, the ALA's primary mission is, in essence, complete. To date, the

ALA has not been able to coalesce the organization around a new cause. This has resulted in a steady decline in revenue, market share, volunteer involvement, and political impact.

Survivability

Survivability is questioned when issues threaten the very existence of the entity. While these issues may be different for various organizations, they frequently are financially based. An organization may realize that it cannot continue to fulfill its mission or serve its constituency without a major influx of funds. This condition may be exacerbated by a loss of volunteer support, reduced donor support, or recent failed attempts at fundraising or capital campaigns. Assuming that the leadership believes the mission is valid, a merger may be a better option than dissolution.

In each of these scenarios describing survivability, viability, and liability, it is clear that a nonprofit organization could spread risk, reduce its debt in relationship to total financial strength, and place itself on firmer financial and organizational footing by considering and completing a merger with a like-minded partner. La Piana (1995) believes that a merger should be considered when "like it or not," a nonprofit group cannot continue to function effectively in pursuit of its mission because inadequate cash flow is crippling operations; a program that accounts for a large percentage of revenue is lost; "a scandal has deprived the group of legitimacy, funding and energy; a board has lost its steam, despite a sustained, competent attempt to revitalize it; or the organization is considering dissolution" (p. 3).

You may readily see that these conditions can be independent or connected, progressive forces compelling a nonprofit organization to merge. Increased liability (political, legal, public, or financial) may lead to questioned viability and result in a position in which survivability of the nonprofit organization becomes doubtful. In light of potential merger negotiations, the position at which your nonprofit organization stands on this three-tiered continuum significantly affects your negotiation posture and

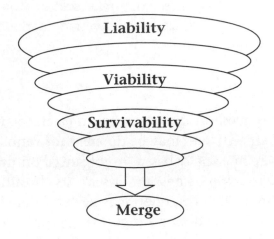

Figure 1–1 The Survivability Spiral

options for merger. Figure 1–1 shows the "survivability spiral," in which organizations decline from liability problems to viability problems, and finally to survivability concerns. In general, the earlier in the survivability spiral the organization approaches merger, the stronger its negotiation posture will be.

STRATEGIC OBJECTIVES

In addition to pinpointing compelling reasons to merge, it is important to develop a list of strategic objectives you wish to accomplish with a merger. These objectives become the rationale behind the decision and outline the specific, anticipated benefits of the merger. By design, the impact of strategic objectives should be quantifiable. These objectives also will become an effective evaluation tool in the postmerger stage, which I will discuss in more detail near the end of the book.

Strategic objectives may be very general or as specific as required by the organization's needs. Your strategic objectives may be borrowed from a strategic plan already in place, or they may come from an ongoing, or new, planning effort. Indeed, recognizing that one or more existing strategic goals of the organization cannot be met in the current organizational makeup may be an impetus to consider merger.

The American Cancer Society (ACS) provides an example of a strategic approach to merger. In 1995, the ACS adopted, among several strategic objectives, a goal to "reduce death from cancer by 50% by the year 2015." A steep decline in volunteer recruitment and flat growth in fundraising efforts signaled to the leadership that the ACS could not reach this goal without realigning its resources. Deciding on an intramerger plan that would collapse state divisions into regional offices allowed the ACS to implement a restructuring strategy that would pave the way toward the original 1995 objective. The ACS realized that putting more resources in the field, focused on education about cancer and patient support, would increase its chance of meeting its goal. The ACS goal was to reduce its chartered divisions, which totaled 56, to 17 by the end of fiscal year 1998. In this example, the strategic objective is being supported through merger. The evaluation of the success is measurable in the realignment of resources (see American Cancer Society—A Case History, Appendix B).

This expectation has been realized in one ACS intramerger: a division with a total staff of 200 shifted people from office jobs to mission delivery jobs and experienced a reduction in administrative staff of 40%, and an increase in field operational (mission delivery) staff of 25%. This is only one example of several strategic objectives that the ACS believed would be better served through a merger that advanced the organization's mission in a socially and fiscally responsible manner. While each organization needs to determine its own specific strategic objectives, some objectives that might be readily addressed through merger include the following:

Provide more constituency service: This concept may take many forms, including something as simple as offering supplementary constituency group insurance or providing free or partially paid educational services. NPOs that have a service component to their membership are always trying to balance membership fees with the serviceable advantages a member receives. Some NPOs eventually reach a point at which the value of the membership services is perceived by a critical mass of members to be worth less than the cost of belonging. At this point, using merger to increase services while holding down membership dues may be an option.

Optimize resources: Frequently, NPOs find a friendly corporation that is trying to attract the same constituencies for similar reasons and in similar ways. An example might be if Greenpeace and an organization like the Sea Shepherd Conservation Society were to merge. By joining forces, the organizations optimize valuable resources. Such a merger could result in sharing mailing lists, strategically determining where environmental actions should be done and by whom, and using the best skills of each organization optimally.

Eliminate duplication of services: This issue is especially prevalent in large organizations with a number of separate corporations operating as mini-NPOs themselves. Leadership's nature is to build infrastructure. In doing so, organizations find that there is significant duplication of services such as printing, fundraising, and warehousing.

Shift resources: Merger, by combining many administrative services, can shift resources (especially human resources) to other critical areas such as constituency service and fundraising.

Expand constituency: If a strategic objective of an organization is to increase its members or constituents, the fastest and most effortless means for a geometric shift may be merger.

Discovering how to service the mission more effectively and more efficiently, and with greater stewardship over the funds, is the most typical way that nonprofits begin to consider a merger. Burkhardt and Sheehan (1995) discuss what is involved in deciding whether or not an organization's mission would be better served through a merger. First, you must determine to what extent the organization is currently fulfilling its mission—its mission accomplishment. You can formulate mission accomplishment by adopting "mission performance measures," which will give you a reliable basis for determining the extent to which you are, or are not, accomplishing your mission. Once you have determined mission accomplishment, the organization can then focus on how merging with another organization can create a new mission statement that all parties can support—this is called mission alignment. This mission alignment needs to go hand in hand with mission accomplishment, and it should allow the key actors in the merging organizations to have a "clear sense of how the combined organizations might achieve greater mission accomplishment than they would if they continued to exist separately" (p. 18).

According to Burkhardt and Sheehan (1995), the last step is the operational assumptions, in which organizations identify and address all the key operational areas of the new, combined organization. "During this phase, the organizations consider how they may take advantage of possible synergies that could exist in the combined organizations" (p. 20). Taking these steps ensures that if the boards of both organizations decide to merge, this decision will be grounded in their raison d'être—their mission. It is through this process that a merger achieves increased capacity.

One note of caution: this in-depth mission examination and mission-related activity assessment can, if made public, expose areas an organization may not wish to become visible. Care must be taken to be objective.

INTEGRATING MERGER GOALS

As you approach the merger decision, you must consider how the strategic objectives and intangible benefits of the merger are integrated with capital rationing and business goals (see Figure 1–2). The strategic objectives of a merger plan are the components of the specific goals that can be accompanied by definite outcomes or measurable (read objective) results. A merger's strategic objectives are defined by the expected merger re-

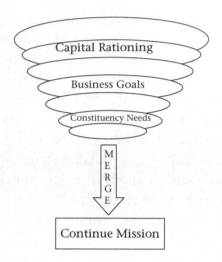

Figure 1–2 Merger Objectives

---

sults that articulate exactly how and how much a merger is expected to help an organization further its mission, provide more responsible stewardship, or better serve its constituency. For example, an organization considering a merger might articulate one of its merger objectives as follows: Enhance public awareness of our mission by increasing our number of volunteers by 40%.

The intangible benefits of the merger are the positive results that cannot be determined or quantified. Therefore, in the example above, the expanded public awareness achieved by having more volunteers is an intangible benefit. A wider constituency base is further developed from greater awareness of the organization in the public arena, and, therefore, the intangible benefit feeds the strategic objective yet again.

Capital rationing deals with economies of scale. Continuing with the same example, it can be seen that a $30 million organization that assigns 10% of its budget to public relations can have a significantly greater impact than a $5 million organization that assigns the same percentage of its budget to public awareness. A merger can pave the way for organizations that share similar missions to work together toward a common cause with greater financial efficiency in almost any category.

Business goals specify how strategic objectives are to be achieved—they are one component of making a strategic goal a reality. Business goals are the financial and administrative decisions necessary for achieving strategic goals. Keeping in mind the example cited above, if the strategic objective of a merger is to increase an organization's public relations effort by 40%, the related business goal might be the following: "Through merging our two-person public relations department with another organization that has four staff members in similar roles, we will be able to handle the increased public relations with only five people and reassign the sixth person." Mergers can be an integral part of business goals and make financial sense by allowing an organization's leaders to better meet their missions through more responsible money management. Remember, a merger is more than simply combining two or more companies. Combining companies will not necessarily achieve any increase in capacity or efficiencies. Merging parties must anticipate and plan for redirecting human, facility, and financial assets if optimal improvement is to be achieved.

Although it is clearly possible to determine a merger's gains in terms of capital rationing and business goals, which can be measured, it is vital to see how they have helped meet the strategic objectives and the intangible benefits of merger, which cannot be quantified as easily. The strategic objectives and intangible benefits are important because nonprofit mergers should be mission-driven mergers that do not necessarily prioritize financial gain ahead of the organization's service goals. However, capital rationing and business goals are important ingredients in any merger consideration because they create an opportunity for a nonprofit entity to increase its capacity to fulfill its mission. Capital rationing and business goals support the strategic objectives and intangible benefits. In the case of the American Cancer Society's intramerger, the creation of stronger merged, interdependent divisions generated increased capacity in a variety of business functions as a result of capital rationing and reduced the need of the national organization to provide some business functions that it had done with limited success based on disparate needs. This financial result makes mergers a vital organizational option.

THE COST OF MERGER

Another facet of merger considerations is the cost of the merger. A merger between nonprofit organizations is akin to changing a tire while driving down the highway. While merger talks (or the merger itself) are under way, all the other daily work, such as board relations, volunteer recruitment and retention, and fundraising efforts must continue. This also is true for mission- and program-related functions, which do not stop during the merger process. Therefore, the cost is twofold: direct monetary costs and human resource costs.

Direct monetary costs usually are centered in three or four areas. Legal costs will vary, depending on many factors including whether the merging entities are organized under the laws of one state or multiple states, membership vs. directorship corporate structure, and documents and filings required by state law. (See Chapter 5 for greater detail.) A merger may also face other legal complexities. In my experience, legal costs can be as low as $3,000 for a simple one-state, two-organization merger, or as high as $30,000 for a very complex merger that involves multiple organizations from many different states.

Consultant fees will vary, depending on the complexity of your merger needs and what type of services you ask a consultant to provide. (See Chapter 7 for more on consultant services.)

Other monetary costs that can be expected with a marriage to another organization are audit fees, severance pay, relocation or moving expenses involved with personnel issues, new logo design and printing costs, web page redesign, and more. The merging entities should also consider any liabilities, such as accrued salaries owed to employees, taxes and penalties, retirement benefits, legal judgments, mortgages, and long-term leases. If the merging organizations are located in different cities or states, the resultant travel cost during and postmerger also must be considered. If a new, or altered, Internal Revenue Service status is required, additional filing costs may be incurred. In most cases, the costs associated with merger are not prohibitive, and the long-range impact can easily outweigh initial costs.

The second type of expense in any merger is the human resource costs, which may be difficult to estimate. The major factors involved in staff time include the following:

Committee meetings and meetings of stakeholders, members, and directors: This may be hard to judge because leadership may not know for sure how many meetings will be required and what level of preparedness will be required to get ready for meetings. Staff and volunteer time will be spent preparing for and attending these meetings.

Negotiating the relationship of the postmerger organization: Negotiations take time and usually teams of people—four days of meetings involving 10 people is 40 days, or approximately two months of lost productivity for that group of staff and volunteers. Plan for that loss.

Securing the required voting percentages: Often, significant staff and volunteer time is spent on personal one-on-one meetings with key leaders to secure their help to move the organization to merger. This takes senior staff away from traditional work. The higher the vote percentage of volunteer directors or membership needed to pass the merger agreement, the more time staff must spend educating members to secure the votes that will allow the merger to pass or succeed. Plan for this time as well.

Remember that a merger will almost always take longer and cost more than originally planned. This is not only because of the major items, such as consultants' fees, attorneys' fees, and severance packages, but also is because of other miscellaneous costs, such as computer/informational system incompatibility, marketing and market position loss, and a melding of publications such as magazines and newsletters produced by the NPOs.

Obviously, completing the merger in a timely matter is a major concern. The longer a merger is delayed, either in negotiations or during the voting stage, the greater the cost will be in all areas. The bottom line is that in planning for costs, be sure to budget with flexibility to allow for extended time and other unknown factors.

REFERENCES

Burkhardt, J. C., & Sheehan, R. M. (1995). *Mission driven mergers*. Cleveland, OH: Association for Research on Nonprofit Organizations and Voluntary Action.

Greif, J. (1990, Summer). Association mergers: Tax and other planning. *The Journal of Taxation of Exempt Organizations*, 32-35.

La Piana, D. (1995). *Nonprofit mergers*. Washington, DC: National Center for Nonprofit Boards.

Lewis, F. C., & Chandler, C. R. (1993, March). The urge to merge: A common-sense approach to association consolidation. *Association Management*, 81-84.

McLaughlin, T. A. (1996). *Seven steps to a successful nonprofit merger*. Washington, DC: National Center for Nonprofit Boards.

Wernet, S. P., & Jones, S. A. (1992). Merger and acquisition activity between nonprofit social service organizations: A case study. *Nonprofit and Voluntary Sector Quarterly, 21*(4), 367-380.

CHAPTER 2

Selecting a Merging Partner

LOOKING FOR CONNECTIONS

THE PREVIOUS CHAPTER explored the rationale that drives organizations toward merger and listed a number of issues that should help a nonprofit organization (NPO) articulate its merger drivers and ask itself questions that will help determine if merger is an appropriate strategy at this time. Additionally, it explored some of the potential costs of merging. It is now time to look at internal issues and process. This process begins with selecting a merger partner.

Choosing a merger partner presents an interesting set of considerations. Merging is not always driven by economics or competitive influences but by many other factors and considerations as well. The key to choosing an appropriate merger partner is always to remain open-minded, think creatively, and focus on long-range results as well as immediate gains. Mergers appear to work better when the parties involved can find an initial connection built on some tangible relationship. Usually, a connection can be categorized within the following relationships: mission, constituency, organization or structure, and geography (see Figure 2–1).

Figure 2–1 Looking for a Merger Partner

Mission Relatedness

Mission relatedness cannot be determined by simply comparing mission statements or looking for key words that are used by both, or all, organizations in the way they characterize themselves. Many organizations may appear to have similar missions but actually be quite different when it comes to the practical implementation of the mission. As an example, the Susan G. Komen Foundation, which focuses on breast cancer, may not be a good merger candidate with Prostate Action, which focuses on prostate cancer, because both have built reputations and constituencies on gender-specific disease. Further, both have corporate support from organizations that cater to gender-specific audiences. Each might be better served by merging with organizations modeled on less disparate constituencies.

Also, many organizations use words in their mission statements to demonstrate their beliefs and values that may or may not accurately reflect how they go about the business of fulfilling their mission. Finally, mission statements are somewhat static: they represent the thinking of the board of directors and staff leadership, who are, or were, influenced by the environmental conditions at a specific point in time. In some cases, policies, procedures, and priorities are changed more often than mission statements are revised.

When exploring mission relatedness with another entity, consider the overall macro-mission concepts over current single issues. For example, if your organization is interested in education (regardless of the specificity), then it makes sense that another educational entity could help further your mission (as you perceive it to be) and might be a potential merger partner. Also, for a health organization whose leadership believes its mission would be furthered by a school-based health initiative, merging with an educational entity already established in a market area of interest might be the most appropriate route to the goal.

Organizational Relatedness

Other potential merging partners may have organizational relatedness. These entities may not share your specific mission concepts, yet they may be good merger candidates because your group is organizationally aligned with them. Organizational alignment does not refer to a specific administrative structure but rather to the philosophical approaches to how business is conducted. One example is two entities whose primary fundraising technique is direct mail. This relatedness would be strengthened if the direct mail efforts were aimed at shared constituencies or even at separate segments of related constituencies. Likewise, several organizations that use special events as a primary fundraising technique may consider a merger if they focus on geographically similar population bases.

It is here that they can take a lesson from their for-profit counterparts. Some for-profit companies are set up in revenue centers that seem, on the surface, to be unrelated, autonomous entities. Some large multinational companies make or sell a large array of seemingly unrelated products and services. The only reason nonprofits do not adopt this profit-center posture is tradition. Breaking with tradition, a number of charities in Beaufort County, SC, found they were all conducting golf tournaments. This, added to a finite population of capable, willing supporters, was beginning to cause donor fatigue, and all the organizations were suffering. As a solution, one single multiday event was created: participants pay a higher fee to play, so the tournament brings in more money, which is then shared among the charities. While this is less than a full merger, it is an example of how creative shifts from traditional parochial NPO posture can improve results. Thinking in these terms can increase a potential list of merger partners.

Last, organizational relatedness may mean that a particular entity has the capacity to handle the organizational, administrative, or operational needs of a potential merging partner. It is important to realize that mergers are not driven only by the needs of a smaller organization that is looking for a larger or stronger partner. A larger partner seeking greater efficiencies also can initiate mergers and increase capacities by aligning with those that are perceived to be smaller or weaker. As an example, Ferris State University in Michigan merged with a small private art and design school in another community. This merger not only provided a consistent financial support base and marketing advantages for the art school but also provided Ferris State University with a well-respected art curriculum, presence, and visibility in a large recruiting and fundraising market.

Constituency Relatedness

This concept is fairly self-explanatory. However, all constituency opportunities might not be obvious at first glance. For example, an environmental organization might focus on another organization with a constituency consisting of individuals with a keen interest in some form of environmental preservation while overlooking a group that might be a better partner because it shares a similar donor, member, or volunteer base. Further exploration by this environmental organization might reveal that a unique constituency, such as catch-and-release fishermen, might be a natural constituency-related group. The operational thrust of all nonprofits is basically the same: To continue to support the mission on a long-term basis, they must continuously identify, recruit, support, and maintain a base of donors, clients, members, and volunteers. With this in mind, constituency can take on a new perspective. For a social service organization that wishes to expand into a specific population or area of the country, an affiliation or merger with one or more entities with access to that population or geography may be the most effective and efficient approach. A basic tenet of advocacy is that more is better. In seeking more political clout, bigger is definitely better.

Geographical Relatedness

Geographical relatedness simply refers to the relationship of organizations based on proximity. Obvious advantages can be achieved by reducing corporate and donor confusion when two organizations are competing for support from the same population segment. However, it is worth mentioning that the geographic boundaries of any particular region are as large or as small as an organization can effectively manage. You might look to nearby towns, counties, and even states for potential merger candidates. If your mission is limited to a certain geographic area, then any entity with specific interest in that geography is a potential merger candidate. For example, if your mission focuses on a natural feature, such as a river, park, or mountain, most organizations that touch, or are touched by, that feature are potential merger partners. Think of a photograph from space that shows the world devoid of state and county boundaries. Sometimes it is helpful for a nonprofit organization to view its world from 100 miles up.

EVALUATING POTENTIAL PARTNERS

Once you identify several, or even just one, organizations that could be potential merging partners, you must begin perhaps the most difficult first step: adjusting your own field of vision. Removal of all emotional barriers that might prevent your organization from considering a merger with another is critical. Most nonprofit organizations are based in a competitive environment. Ironically, the most likely merger candidates may very well be organizations that you have previously viewed as your "competition" for dollars, donors, and volunteers. One example would be the merger between the two largest national hunger relief organizations: Foodchain and Second Harvest (Chronicle of Philanthropy, 2000). Or the best candidate may be a similar organization in a related field that your organization has made a consistent effort to eschew.

Therefore, the first step in evaluating possible merger candidates is to drop preconceived values and rejection points concerning organizations that are similar to your own. This is an area in which a consultant can be of great value. La Piana (1995) believes that a consultant can help you identify a potential partner by organizing a search, helping you articulate what you are looking for in a potential partner, and outlining what you hope to accomplish by a merger. Also, a consultant can independently ascertain an accurate interest that one or more merger partners may have in a merger without your organization initiating an approach.

It is important to remember the ultimate result the merger is expected to achieve (see Figure 2–2). In most cases, it is the furthering of the mission. Nonprofit mergers are more like common-interest developments than takeover bids. The notion is to combine resources that affect the mission of each organization in a positive way, where both are served and create a larger picture, much like a mosaic. This "mission mosaic" is like the tilework it represents. Individual tiles (read missions) are assembled in a way that presents a picture in which the one organization is greater for the common good. Upon close inspection individual missions may still be clearly defined while contributing to the whole.

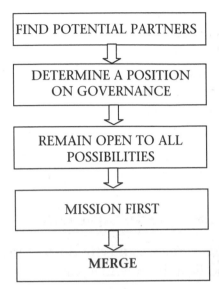

Figure 2–1 Getting Ready To Merge

The second step in evaluating possible partners is almost as difficult as the first: You must be aware of your position on important merger issues. Governance, leadership, and organizational structure are the critical items on the minds of most volunteers. Other issues may arise, but experience suggests they are connected to these three essential issues. For the reasons previously mentioned, it might be helpful to think of merger as marriage rather than a competition with a winner and loser. Mergers are unions, not federations; therefore, your merger position is a point on a continuum of these merger issues. Your position on the continuum will sometimes be determined by the drivers mentioned in Chapter 1. Evaluating your position on this continuum at the beginning of the process and reconsidering it after a few months of merger exploration, education, and consideration usually results in a significantly different placement. Where you and your volunteers are on day one should change with time and discussion. Be aware of your position on the three key issues, but don't adopt a rigid position too early. More will be presented on this topic in Chapter 4.

The third step in evaluation is to remain open to all possible merger outcomes until they are abandoned or deemed impracticable. Negative attitudes or assumptions can prevent your organization from venturing into new territory that could expand its horizons. Negative assumptions, such as "There is no way they would merge with us," "A merger with them would be akin to organizational suicide," or "A merger is the survival of the fittest," impair the development of creative options. The reality is that until discussions are held and governance, structure, and asset allocation are discussed, you cannot assume there is no way to make a merger work.

MEASURING SIMILARITIES AND DIFFERENCES

After overcoming governance and emotional barriers, it's time to consider the practical aspects of the potential partner(s) organization. Below is a list of considerations and questions that you may want to explore:

- Do we share a similar mission?

- Do we share a similar, or the same, constituency?

- Do we have a similar operational style?

- How do we compare in organizational size?

- How do we compare geographically?

- Do we each share a similar kind of public image? Is one of us better or less well known?

- Are we seen in a similar light within our industry or field? (equal professional perception)

- Are we in similar financial positions in real dollars?

- Do we each have facilities that are important to our mission?

- What assets can we bring, and what assets can we acquire, through merging with this organization, and vice versa?

- How will we increase capacity overnight?

These questions are not designed to be a yes or no filter but rather simply to suggest an array of considerations. For example, the question on geography will have a different connotation if you are trying to grow outside your present boundaries than if your strategic objective is to reduce competition. Choosing a merging partner is not about competition, it is about the resultant team. The best mergers evolve into a total that is greater than the sum of the parts, whether they are measured in resultant financial terms or in potential mission enhancement outcomes.

Once a determination is made on a suitable merger partner, approach it carefully. The same barriers to merger that you may have overcome in your own thinking may need to be confronted in others. "Approach a potential merger partner respectfully, in a manner that allows its leaders to save face and maintain their share of control of the situation. The merger process melds the mission, culture and identity of both groups into the new entity. Fear of change, loss of autonomy, ego, habit and culture cause non-profits to avoid mergers" (La Piana, 1995, p. 20). Failure to achieve mergers because of ego or other emotion-laden issues is contrary to the long-term commitment to your mission.

An example: A nonprofit organization identified two potential partners with which to merge. Partner A was geographically closer. Partner B was smaller but financially sound. Merging all three entities was not an option. All three entities were solvent but were aware that a merger could increase each organization's mission capacity.

The merging entity scheduled a presentation to its board of directors by each potential partner. Partner A presented a well-developed presentation focused on the financial advantages and potential impact of a merger. Partner B presented an image based on relationships and a more humanistic approach to joining forces.

The merging entity chose B.

This example is just one of many that demonstrates how NPOs' merger decisions are frequently based more on emotion than on other factors. The organizational leaders in the example above voted with their hearts, not their heads. They chose to ignore some financial and operational advantages in favor of relationship. It is difficult to tell which decision would have served them best. Sometimes operational opportunities for autonomy might be preferred over a strict financial pro forma.

REFERENCES

Chronicle of Philanthropy, May 4, 2000.

La Piana, D. (1995). *Nonprofit mergers*. Washington, DC: National Center for Nonprofit Boards.

CHAPTER 3

Laying the Groundwork with Staff and Volunteers

CONSIDERING HUMAN ELEMENTS

PREVIOUS CHAPTERS HAVE DISCUSSED mergers from business and mission perspectives, but the planning of all issues must be considered in light of the human resource and personnel aspects of all organizations. One unique aspect of most nonprofit organizations (NPOs) is the breadth of volunteer leadership, members, and staff who are emotionally dedicated and committed to the mission of the organization. Most staff members consider themselves to be in-part volunteers—that is, they feel more connected to the organization than merely as employees. Recognizing this human, emotional connection is essential to the long-term health of NPOs, but frequently it can be an impediment to the change process required for a successful merger. Resistance to change, especially if the organization is successful, can be a major obstacle in completing a merger.

Even if the executive management and board members are convinced that a merger will allow for greater and more efficient mission accomplishment, they must consider the human aspects of the merger. It is clear that mergers have a direct impact on personnel, and that impact is very often a negative one. Despite leadership's best efforts to promote a new vision for the organization, staff members often fear a loss of organizational independence and identity and view merger as the death of an organization they care about deeply (La Piana, 1995, p. 18).

STARTING AT THE TOP: THE CHIEF EXECUTIVE OFFICER (CEO)

To begin to deal with change resistance, start at the top. If the CEO of any of the organizations involved is not convinced a merger is an appropriate direction, the odds of fulfilling the potential of, or even completing, the merger are not good. In working with CEOs, keep in mind that you are addressing not only the CEO, but his or her supporters as well. CEOs are rarely isolated from boards of directors; after all, it's usually the board of directors that hires the CEO. Most CEOs have a core group of directors who will look out for their interests. Planning for the CEO's future will definitely influence the outcome of the early merger talks and can either impede or smooth the way to a merger. It is strongly recommended that if one of the current CEOs is to be the eventual chief executive, the appointment be made early in the negotiation process, unless other political influences indicate otherwise. When two or more CEOs are waiting in line for the top position of the merged organization, you must resolve the issue quickly and decisively.

Lewis and Chandler (1993) suggest that one of the executives ought to assume the overall direction of the organization as chief executive officer and the other should take responsibility for day-to-day operation as the chief operating officer. But even in this scenario, there "should be only one number one" (p. 90). McLaughlin (1996) proposes another solution: Let the chief executives work out the question of leadership among themselves and allow the merged board to decide whether to approve the decision. He also states that sometimes it's not the job that the individuals want to retain, but the prestige, the salary, or the autonomy, or all three. "If that is the case, it may be possible to structure a position in the new entity that will meet those needs" (p. 11). McLaughlin also suggests that the boards of each organization discover if the chief executives have employment contracts that may require the attention of a lawyer if they are to be adjusted.

In some cases, early selection of a CEO may create political problems. Some mergers in which the CEO was selected at the premerger stage resulted in the new, merged board feeling that one of its chief responsibilities had been usurped. This issue is delicate, and the selection and timing of the announcement to all players is extremely important.

If no clear resolution is reached as to which, if either, of the current CEOs will become the new leader, the newly merged board can then open the position. In this case, organizations sometimes will first limit the applicants to current staff and sometimes open the search to other candidates. Either option is acceptable.

PRELIMINARY MEETING OF CEOs

Initially, preliminary meetings with the CEOs of all parties involved should be held individually to address interpersonal issues. Interpersonal issues related to the merger fall into two categories: job-related issues and issues that affect the individual's personal life. Both must be addressed. Professional issues that need to be resolved with the CEOs may include increased responsibility, increased travel, job title, reporting network, liability issues, salary, benefits, office space, identification and number of support staff, input into timing and process of merger, and, in some cases, retirement planning. Personal issues include office location, relocation obligations, increased travel, hours dedicated to work, and job security. The merger consultant must discuss and resolve as many of these questions as early in the merger process as possible. The expected outcome is that each CEO will accept the changes in job and personal life that the pending merger will bring.

These preliminary meetings with the merging CEOs should be held individually, and in private, to address and relieve as many concerns as possible. Lewis and Chandler (1993) believe that it is vital that the top executives meet early in the process "and attempt to establish a close working relationship" (p. 89). In all cases, some compromise must occur.

After the individual meetings are held, the chief administrators of each merging entity should meet with the consultant or facilitator to begin to explore the methodology behind the upcoming changes. A chart identifying the meetings and expected outcomes is presented in Table 3–1.

These meetings may include more than one staff person from each nonprofit organization, but should reflect equal representation. One entity should not bring an entourage, while another is represented by only one or two people.

Also, this is not the time to involve agents or legal representation in the process. If the negotiations result in a merger, there will be plenty of time to adopt legal and organizational protective postures. Singer and Yankey (1991) suggest that you use these initial, informal meetings to allow for conversations and collegiality to develop naturally (p. 360). McLaughlin (1996) believes that you also can build trust between the organizations by "agreeing to consult with your partner on every major financial, programmatic, or personnel decision" (p. 7). Also, he says, make sure to be "equitable in the choice of meeting sites" (p. 7). Some organizations fear that an unforeseen event will prevent one or more of their representatives from attending a meeting and push to allow alternates in the negotiations process. Because of the history-building nature of relationships and negotiation points, alternates should not be allowed into the negotiations once they have begun.

The initial meetings should focus on the compelling reasons to merge, the barriers or impediments to merger, and each organization's needs and wishes that must be addressed before the merger can occur. This also is the appropriate time for sharing information about each organization that will be helpful in determining the ultimate merger structure, such as membership and constituency information, cultural specifics, history, and

Table 3–1 Typical Meeting Schedule Leading to Merger

Meeting	Attendees	Agenda/Outcome
1	CEOs of All Organizations	Learn about organizations. Explore merger concept and parameters
2	Individual CEOs	Determine their support and iron out early interpersonal issues
3	CEOs Key Board Leadership	Present merger idea, get input regard--ing their support and interests
4	CEOs, Senior Staff, and 2-3 key volunteers from all organizations (Merger Design Team)	Have preliminary merger talks on major issues of governance, control, leadership, and finance
5	Merge Design Team	Have continual talks toward agreement on the terms of merger
6	CEOs, Senior Staff, Volunteer Leaders, and all Board Members	Hold individual private meetings with each organization's board of directors to present the merger concept and get approval to proceed
7	Merger Design Team	Report on individual organizational meetings and negotiate concerns of the respective boards of directors
8	CEO, Senior Staff, Board of Directors (individual organization)	Report on outcomes of negotiations and get a "straw" vote to proceed
9	Merger Design Team	Report on straw vote outcome, modify insubstantial issues, review draft plan and agreement to merge, bylaws and other documents
10	Board of Directors of each organization	Initial vote(s) (see notice requirement chart in Appendix B)

financial overviews. This also is the time to raise the issues that each organization feels most strongly about—these potential deal breakers must be brought to the table and discussed early on. As these items are explored, a catharsis usually occurs among attendees that removes some of the strong reaction and makes the issues seem less volatile. Someone once said that we go crazy en masse but come to reason one at a time. Addressing the deal-breaker topics is crucial to the future of the merger. Lewis and Chandler (1993) note that "nothing could be more devastating than to spend months successfully negotiating minor issues, only to discover irreconcilable differences at the last moment" (p. 89).

BUILDING SUPPORT: VOLUNTEER LEADERSHIP

Prior to any meeting involving volunteers, each CEO should at least discuss the possibilities of merger with the volunteer and staff leadership in his or her organization. Likewise, if other merger partners initially approach an NPO executive, his or her first response should be to confidentially notify a small component of the volunteer leadership on the board of directors. Failure to do so could put the executive in a bad light in the future.

At the initial meeting of the merging parties (see Table 3–1, Meeting 1), each organization should be prepared to discuss documented evidence of its current organizational structure and health. This information should include, at a minimum, recent information describing the mission and goals of the organization, current financial statements, lists of major assets, current and expected liabilities existing or potential litigation, bylaws, articles of incorporation, and a strategic plan (if one exists). Exchanging this information before the meeting is usually helpful. There is no need to show great detail or reveal new strategies, but the more open the parties are with each other, the better.

Volunteer leaders from your board of directors are the absolute keys to a smooth merger. These are the elected, appointed, or perceived volunteer powers that actually move the organization. All organizations have them. They must be identified and brought in early if merger is to occur.

Think of your volunteer leadership in the context of not only the elected leaders of your organization but also those who wield considerable influence over your organization. Every organization has a subset of leaders who can influence the vote and attitude of the volunteers or board members. These "supervolunteers" frequently provide the key to any merger or other major organizational shift. Identify this group early and begin to explore their interests, concerns, and attitudes about a potential merger. They will ultimately provide the political power to make the merger succeed.

In this process, think about who within the organization (staff or volunteer) will be the best person to contact these supervolunteers and develop a strategy to do so. One usually successful technique is to use the supervolunteers as inside salespeople. Sometimes, they can have the merger vote in hand conceptually long before the voting day arrives.

In one nonprofit merger, the group was pleased to discover that one member had obtained enough proxies to secure the vote before the meeting. Many organizations do not allow proxies. This one did, and it worked in its favor.

Using volunteers to influence other volunteers will also serve to remove some of the focus of the issue from senior management. Yet another advantage of this tactic is discovering potential barriers to merger early on in the process. This alone will be invaluable as the merger vote nears.

INVOLVING VOLUNTEER LEADERSHIP

Following the first meetings of the CEOs, a meeting of volunteer leaders should be held to report the results of the CEOs' meetings. These meetings should be held independently for all organizations (see Table 3–1, Meeting 2). The volunteer leadership should be board members with the ability to influence the board of directors' votes, if possible (see Table 3–1,

Meeting 3). To help volunteers put things in perspective, try starting the volunteer leaders meeting by having each participant say why he or she is a volunteer and why he or she believes the work of the organization is important. This process takes the emphasis back to mission and away from personal agendas. The sharing of statements by all present who wish to speak that express interest in participating in merger deliberations, an organizational overview presented by each entity, and an open time for questions and concerns also may be effective as icebreakers.

The goal of the volunteer leaders meeting should be to formulate a joint statement announcing that the parties are proceeding with merger discussions and agreeing to meet at a specific future date. It is important to have a consultant present at the volunteer leaders meeting to help keep the focus on the merger issues, rather than emotional issues, and, more important, to answer early technical and procedural questions (see Chapter 7 for information about working with consultants and other professionals). The volunteer leaders meeting should also provide an answer to the following questions: (1) Does the leadership wish to continue exploring the merger concept? and (2) What should be the process of notifying the remaining board members? Carefully recording the minutes of this volunteer leadership meeting, including the notation of motions, seconds, and votes, if any, in which the CEO is instructed to continue to pursue the merger process is imperative. The CEO needs to avoid the scenario in which he or she outruns the volunteer leadership in an issue of this magnitude. Moving too far down the path of merger without support of influential board members could result in loss of confidence in the CEO's ability to lead.

The next meetings of the merging parties should include CEOs as well as a contingent of the key leadership of both organizations (see Table 3–1, Meetings 4 and 5). A team of three people from each merging partner seems to work best.

Each team needs to be similar in size and be vested with similar authority to act on behalf of their organizations. The process will be hindered if one team has decision-makers and leaders and the other does not (see a discussion of how to form a design team later in this chapter).

These meetings should be a review of the events of the past talks and meetings and are designed to educate the leadership. It is important to avoid the circumstance in which a team of all volunteers or staff feels they cannot go forward without gathering input from their volunteer or staff counterparts. Therefore, each team must feel empowered to speak on behalf of the board of directors with reasonable belief that the board will accept their recommendations.

Following these meetings, and assuming the volunteer leadership is prepared to move forward, a strategy should be set in place to educate the remaining board members and membership of the organization. At this point, the rumor mill is often operating at full tilt, but it should not be addressed in any formal or public way until the board of directors is fully informed of the issues. To do otherwise would be to outrun the directors' responsibilities and would be inappropriate.

McLaughlin (1996) offers these tips when dealing with communication in early merger discussions (p. 18):

- Initially, keep the idea among management and the board.

- Involve the staff and middle management after the leadership question is resolved so the merger development issue and the leadership question can be announced as part of the package.

- Involve staff and take your time with the process rather than rush it through.

- Give staff the chance to buy into the process because, while mergers may start from the top and work down, they are only successful from the ground up.

- Tell the truth if a premature announcement of merger discussions has leaked out.

- Don't forget to informally approach foundations, corporations, and other groups or individuals that contribute substantial funds or otherwise have a vested interest to the organizations to alleviate their potential concerns and gain support for the proposal.

In addition, it is a good idea to notify any major accounts payable, lien holders, or mortgage holders of the pending merger. In some states not having prior approval of merger by mortgage holders may delay the effective date of a merger.

GETTING BUY-IN: THE BOARD OF DIRECTORS

The first real political fireworks may begin when the board of directors is approached with the notion of merger (see Table 3–1, Meeting 6). It is critical that your leadership work the halls to have personal contact with all directors prior to the mailing of a meeting notice that mentions that merger discussion is on the agenda. "Working the halls" has become an expression indicating that nonprofit directors are prepared to make many of the critical decisions necessary to run the organization by talking with other board members outside of the context of an actual meeting. Mergers are frequently so politically charged that working the halls is an imperative, not an option. Of course, this may allow some directors to organize an oppositional thrust, but that cannot be helped. If the responsible parties of a nonprofit organization do not feel merger is in the organization's best interest, even after they are presented with the opportunity and educated about its benefit based on strong supporting evidence, the merger will probably not be approved. This is the time for strong executive leadership to emerge. The CEO should carry the banner and ensure that subordinates are not undermining the efforts of the leadership. Patience is an ally. Don't rush. Work closely with your merger partner(s) and set timing in the best interest of both parties. Consider whether the process should continue in a parallel time frame or if one party moving first would assist closure (see Table 3–1, Meeting 7).

Ideally, the outcome of the first meeting of the full board of directors when merger is discussed ought to be the adoption of a resolution to continue merger talks and deliberations (see Table 3–1, Meeting 8). While this resolution will not be binding from a legal perspective, it will officially sanction the leadership's future merger activities and will serve to instill the strong possibility of merger in the minds of the board of directors. It also will give the CEO an indication of the general support, or lack of support, for the notion of merger. A further outcome of this meeting should be the appointment of a design team or oversight committee to represent each merging organization in further discussions regarding merger and to bring back a report of recommendations (see Table 3–1, Meeting 9).

Board buy-in is essential because the board of directors will be required to vote the merger up or down. More important, the amount of board buy-in required will vary from state to state. Some states may recognize a vote of a simple majority (50%) of directors to effect a merger while others may require as much as a two-thirds majority. This number could be even higher if the vote is taken in writing or by proxy rather than in a meeting. This issue is discussed more fully in Chapter 5.

The goal should be to achieve 100% support. Volunteer organizations will be better served if they move into merger with the significant support of their membership and directorship. A simple majority vote, while it may result in the desired merger, may cause a huge rift in the organization and its leadership. To increase buy-in, work to find concepts that will help volunteers see the advantages and opportunities a merger can bring (see Table 3–1, Meeting 10).

CREATING THE MERGER DESIGN TEAM

A merger design team should be formed with an equal number of decision-makers representing each participating organization. This team will meet to officially begin the merger talks. The issues of greatest interest to merger design teams usually include the following:

- Governance and organizational representation
- Senior staff leadership
- Organizational structure (directorship vs. membership) and voting rights of each party
- Impact of merger on national affiliations
- Effective date of the merger
- Survivorship of merged corporation
- Impact on field support and other staff
- Bylaws and various internal processes protected through bylaws
- Perception that smaller groups will lose identity and autonomy
- Perception that larger groups will have to absorb the expenses of smaller or less solvent participants

It is not practical to venture a prediction as to how long meetings will be or how many meetings the design team will hold. This process will vary with a multitude of individual and organizational considerations. Some merger talks are completed in one meeting, and some extend a year or more. Suffice it to say that all mergers are unique, and that each design team needs to establish its own working pace. Some merger design teams organize work groups around the major points listed above or other issues that emerge. Critical deal-breaker issues such as governance should be decided by a team with very influential members representing all interested parties. Your design team will become your primary sales force to help other volunteers accept the merger conditions. Make sure the right people are at the table. A typical design team includes:

- Chief executive officer
- Chief operations officer
- Chief financial officer

- Current president or chair of the organization (see Table 3–1, Meeting 4)

Individuals with expertise in merger and merger-related issues as well as influential volunteers are good choices for selection to the design team. Some organizations even include volunteers or board members they expect to be opposed to a merger in order to get that perspective at the negotiation table.

SPREADING THE WORD: WORKING WITH VOLUNTEERS AND STAFF

The important thing accomplished during the negotiation process by the design team is getting your key staff and volunteers comfortable with the realities and process of merger. This will ensure that they will enthusiastically provide the leadership, with the rest of the board of directors and membership to support the merger when it is time to vote.

The staff needs to make a continued effort with volunteers to move the process forward. As with all good public relations efforts, the NPO's informational efforts should begin within the organization. A staff meeting to handle rumor control and ongoing written updates to staff and all volunteers (especially those not close to the merger deliberations) are necessities. The information process doesn't need to be costly or fancy, but it does need to be consistent and frequent. When you are contemplating or planning a merger, "it is not possible to overcommunicate" with your staff, according to Lewis and Chandler (1993, p. 91). To avoid unneeded stress on their part, let your staff and supporters know that major changes as a result of the merger may take six months to a year, or more, to complete. Reassure them that they need not fear that there will be an immediate wave of layoffs, job description changes, or staff reassignments, unless these are part of the planned initial strategic outcomes. Let them know how they will be involved in the decision-making processes regarding any major structural changes. In a nonprofit, volunteer-driven, mission-focused entity, a merger will not succeed if its people power is disregarded or alienated.

Good communication is key, but as McLaughlin (1996) recognizes, "Exactly what constitutes 'good communication' differs according to the situation. The trick is to understand what type of communication is needed, to whom, and when" (p. 18).

Announcement of the merger can have a negative impact on many staff members. Those considering leaving the organization before the merger notice are likely to leave shortly after the announcement. Further, others will worry about job loss or changes in their working environment. Lewis and Chandler (1993) explain that "employees feel some sense of loss even if they retain their jobs. Fight this with staff social functions, joint staff task forces for problem resolution, and a lot of reassurance and hand-holding, particularly during the transition period" (p. 90). Senior staff should be reassured of their job status, but also provided with honest assessments of the current situation. Some organizations even establish a merger hot line to call for answers to immediate questions. Organization-wide e-mail or an e-mail response center also is an excellent way to communicate. Your consultant can be an important asset in fielding and responding to questions and concerns, as well as in providing a buffer between various constituencies and the organizational leadership.

Spend time addressing the human concerns and fears that naturally arise out of merger talks. Good communication can help staff members avoid making an emotionally based decision to leave the organization without knowing all the facts. You do not want to get into the old paradigm of "I've made up my mind, don't trouble me with the facts!" Make sure your workers get the facts first.

SEIZING ORGANIZATIONAL OPPORTUNITIES

One other major element in mergers—one that is often overlooked—is the opportunity to effect sweeping organizational change. The merger will often give birth to the notion that there must be a change of everything and anything organizationally or operationally related to the nonprofit entity. This idea provides fertile ground for significant operational shifts. New initiatives such as zero-based budgeting, decommissioning programs of questionable value, and opening or closing facilities are frequently easier to accomplish in the process of a merger. Work with volunteers and staff should focus on the positive side and the long-range vision of the merger and emphasize their investment in the big picture. Just as photographs from space show no boundaries on land between states and countries, a wide and expansive view of organizations can allow for one grand vision that can unify disparate people, programs, and priorities.

Any reassurance that can be given to senior and essential staff during the early aspects of merger will be helpful. Staff stress is high during these times. Merger hearsay suggests that there will be massive staff shifts and even potential reduction of staff post-merger. Work to combat this perception unless it is the planned reality. Further, assume that any information provided to staff will be shared with volunteers and vice versa. Experience shows that the close nature typical in NPOs between staff and volunteers will promote a fluid flow of information even if senior management directs otherwise.

REFERENCES

La Piana, D. (1995). *Nonprofit mergers*. Washington, DC: National Center for Nonprofit Boards.

Lewis, F. C., & Chandler, C. R. (1993, March). The urge to merge: A common-sense approach to association consolidation. *Association Management*, 81–84.

McLaughlin, T. A. (1996). *Seven steps to a successful nonprofit merger*. Washington, DC: National Center for Nonprofit Boards.

Singer, M. I., & Yankey, J. A. (1991). Organizational metamorphosis: A study of eighteen nonprofit mergers, acquisitions, and consolidations. *Nonprofit Management & Leadership, 1*(4), 357–369.

CHAPTER 4

Negotiating and Determining Structure

OVERALL CONTEXT OF NEGOTIATING

NEGOTIATING AND DETERMINING GOVERNANCE structure are presented together because in my experience the two are inexorably joined when moving nonprofit organizations (NPOs) to merger. In for-profit mergers, issues of negotiation tend to center around money. Issues of book value, long- and short-term debt, market share, profitability, and shareholder relations are of major concern. In publicly held companies, what Wall Street investment analysts think must be considered as well. While some of these issues are germane in NPO mergers, the more common negotiating points are focused on governance, control, representation, and the ultimate authority of volunteers. Negotiations for NPO mergers are more about bylaws than balance sheets. Further, NPO mergers are not as much about financial discovery as they are about open sharing of information and needs.

As mentioned earlier, in my experience, the negotiating process in NPO mergers centers on three areas: governance, leadership, and organizational structure.

Governance

Governance is self-explanatory: it refers to who will ultimately have authority over the organization. It is a major factor because NPOs all have boards of directors that have fiduciary responsibilities with the entities they serve. These board members frequently are not willing to give up control easily. Most of these problems will be resolved in design team meetings but will be a significant consideration in merger negotiations (Governance is explored later in this chapter in a section titled "Developing an effective governance model.")

Leadership

Leadership is about governance but has several unique issues that frequently appear as negotiation items. Unless the organizations are of equal size and strength, usually one merging partner wishes to maintain the "higher ground" of leadership when the organizations merge. Organizational culture frequently presents barriers to the merger. One example of this is an organization in which there is a cultural or bylaws-protected progression of chairs to the top volunteer post (e.g., the second vice chair becomes first vice chair, then chair-elect, then chair). Sometimes volunteers have positioned themselves for years to assume this position. They are not always quick to give up the opportunity for leadership in a merged environment. Your organization may have other, even more complex, leadership issues. Do not ignore them. They can become deal breakers.

Organizational structure refers to the staffing patterns that will occur post-merger. Nonprofit executives frequently have forged relationships with their volunteers that provide them with some protection and consideration. These issues are also critical in negotiations.

Do not assume that staff and volunteer allegiance is reserved for the most senior levels of your organization. Any staff that routinely meets with or communicates directly with volunteers probably will have more volunteer influence than you might originally guess. Expect volunteers and staff to communicate regularly on merger issues. This fact suggests that accurate and consistent communication among all parties is critical.

In preparation for merger negotiations you may be well served to evaluate where your organization fits on the critical issues mentioned above (see Figure 4–1).

The point at which you and your organization's leadership fall on the continuum, in relationship to the suggested negotiation barriers, is an indicator of how much effort in education and negotiation will be required to effect the merger.

As mentioned earlier, the first step is to begin with a free and open exchange of financial, membership, and operational data so that each party can begin to understand the relative position the other occupies. Attempting to extrapolate these data into a weakness that may be moving one or more entities to merger is not productive. The overriding consideration of

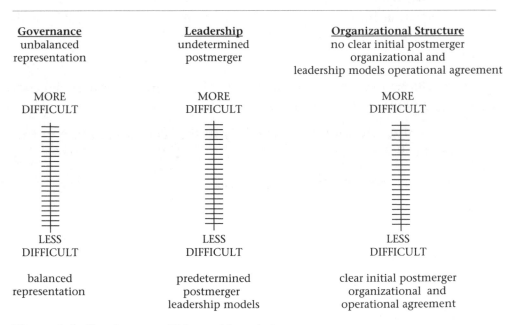

Figure 4–1 Continuum of Merger Negotiations

merger is to increase capacity, not to prey on a real or perceived weakness of one or more merger partners. In almost all instances, all partners bring to the potential merger those activities in which they excel. This is what makes the partnership more powerful.

The next step is to ensure that the design team representatives know what the expectations of their organization are. Specifically, they must know the limits beyond which they may not go without group approval. You will learn in the technical section of this book (Chapter 6) that before a merger is consummated, your board, and possibly your membership, will be required to vote to ratify it. If your negotiations have resulted in a plan of merger that is outside the acceptance parameters of the leadership and members, the merger vote may fail.

For example, if your organization is twice the size of a merger partner and your leadership indicates that they will not merge unless the resultant board of directors has a majority of representation from the larger entity, then put this fact on the negotiation table. My experience in merger negotiations is that if reasonable people are involved, they are usually willing to compromise if the point is perceived to be for the good of the whole.

Each merger negotiation has a unique set of discussion parameters but may include any or all of the following:

- State of survivability (defined fully in the technical section of this book)

- Facilities (opening or closing of office, etc.)

- Operational headquarters (location and capacity)

- Protection of sacred cows (programs, activities, or other political/environmental attachments)

- Volunteer and member representation

- Governance

Orchestrating the beginning of the merger process can do much to establish a tone that will assist the talks throughout the process. Because organizations are not being taken over, the hostile atmosphere that can surround for-profit mergers rarely exists. For the most part, the participating organizations choose to become part of the discussion. This point should be emphasized with the group.

The spirit of the negotiating process should be collegial. NPO mergers are seeking to combine resources toward an end to developing a better opportunity to impact mission, not take advantage of another organization. If design team members begin to feel the negotiation process is anything less, barriers will come up and the road to success will be harder and take longer.

Some suggestions regarding beginning merger talks are presented below:

- Take time to socialize the group. Help them to get to know each other on a personal basis as a way to minimize turf issues and establish an air of collegiality for future deliberations.

- Pick a spokesperson who has an inclusive, nonthreatening style. Nonprofit organization merger talks are not about protection and confrontation, they are about seeking cooperative advantages.

- Place less controversial points on the agenda before more controversial points to build a relationship.

- Demonstrate your understanding that positions taken by negotiating team members are not personal but are rather their perception of what they think is best for their organization.

- Try to determine if difficult negotiation points are supported by a large contingency of the organization or are shared by only a few.

- Determine if negotiating points are based on fact or perception. Facts can be negotiated; perceptions cannot.

Last, remember that emotions will diminish as points are rationally discussed. Issues that seem confrontational and major hurdles may soften when discussed, reviewed, and discussed at a later time.

MIXING MEMBERSHIPS AND DIRECTORSHIPS

One major consideration when beginning negotiations is to address volunteer involvement pre- and post-merger. Nonprofit corporations usually have one of two basic types of nonprofit organization structures: one is directorship; the other is membership. "Directorship" means that the responsibilities of the corporation rest with the board of directors, which is usually self-perpetuating (board members elect themselves to the board). "Membership" usually means that a group of people who meet certain criteria are entitled to some rights and responsibilities to the corporation. One of those rights frequently is acting on corporate issues such as election of directors or officers and the adoption and administration of bylaws. Some states require that memberships vote to approve merger.

Directorship corporations may have classes of directors who are not permitted to vote on corporate issues and therefore have no control. One can easily see that mergers between two or more entities with different structures cause an interesting dilemma.

If all parties to a merger are directorships with no members who are enfranchised to effect corporate policy, the resultant merged structure will probably be a directorship, and negotiation will center on how many directors from each merging party will govern the new operation.

If, on the other hand, the merging parties have both a directorship and a membership structure and they want to make the resultant corporation a directorship, there may be additional obstacles to overcome. No matter how your organization operated in the past, if it is a membership corporation, state statutes may require you to obtain membership approval, via a formal vote, to merge (see Chapter 6 for more details like this). In some cases approval may be required by as much as two-thirds of the total number of members. It's easy to see that if you are faced with asking your volunteer membership to vote away their rights as members, you have much work to do.

In one merger completed among four similar organizations in four separate states, all but one entity was a membership corporation. The resultant corporation was expected to be a directorship corporation. The total number of directors in the four merging corporations was 110 people. The total number of membership (with voting rights) was 245. The resultant board of directors had 20 members (five from each state). While this case may be a bit extreme, it is not unusual in membership nonprofit corporation mergers. In essence, the merger cited above asked 335 people to vote themselves out of franchisement as it relates to nonprofit corporate governance.

The complexities of the process of getting members and directors to vote themselves out of their positions could easily fill another book. A design team schedule to begin discussion on these types of issues is described in Exhibit 4–1. Some key points in addressing this issue are mentioned below:

- Have legal counsel review your bylaws and state statutes to determine exactly who has the authority to vote on a merger. (Note: If your bylaws are suspended, unless the suspension expressly requires a membership vote to reinstate, you may need to revert to presuspended language.)

- Communicate with all those who have authority to vote (directors and members) as early in the process as possible. This can usually be started as soon as your directors have indicated tacit or straw vote approval to proceed. Remind them of their continued importance to the organization.

- Make sure your communications focus on mission enhancement, capacity increase, and stewardship.

Exhibit 4–1 Design Team Schedule

Month 1
- Assemble design team
- Select volunteer members
- Determine meeting schedule and pick venue
- Gather pertinent data about your organization
- Disseminate and review data re: merger partners

Month 2
- First team meeting to determine outside negotiating parameters
- First meeting of all teams
- Establish schedule for future meetings
- Set agenda for next meeting

Month 3
- Second meeting of all teams
- Begin to get closure (sign-off) on specific negotiation points
- Update board of directors on progress
- Develop list of early stumbling points

Month 4
- Third meeting of all teams
- Governance issues should be close to settlement
- Senior staff issues resolved if possible
- Begin discussion re: facilities and other essential operational issues
- If merger looks imminent, begin staff information stream

Month 5
- Develop plan and agreement to merge
- Bylaws language agreed upon re: governance
- Schedule meetings with full boards to discuss merger options
- Develop a calendar for voting (see Appendix I)
- End of meetings with design teams

- Establish a meaningful way—through committees, councils, or other official venues—for volunteers to stay connected and, more important, provide input to the new, merged entity.

- Hold local or regional information sessions.

- Identify pockets of resistance, and use staff and supportive volunteers to reduce the resistance.

The most successful programs to prevent volunteer disenfranchisement are those that develop a clear plan to deal with the issue before the effective date of the merger. When asked the question, "I was a voting member, what's going to happen to me after the merger?" you and your leadership must be prepared with an answer.

DEVELOPING AN EFFECTIVE GOVERNANCE MODEL

In most mergers in which I have worked, governance is by far the most contested issue. In a few cases, all parties come to the table with similar strengths, wealth, size, and so forth and agree from the start to equal representation, but that is rare. The philosopher John Donne said, "Laws are created by the weak to protect them from the strong." Never is this more evident than in governance discussion when merging nonprofit organizations. Larger organizations, either in financial resources or membership size, often perceive that it is a natural outcome of merger that they will either control the resultant entity or at least have a more significant voice. Entities perceived as smaller in any respect tend to fear they will be swallowed up, consumed, and regulated into an unimportant component of the larger organization. When these concerns arise, compromise is the key.

Although most organizations choose to create a self-perpetuating board of directors, there are some instances in which it is not appropriate for a board to be self-perpetuating. It is possible that a self-perpetuating board could damage the organization's image or drive away members who may feel they are not adequately represented. Similarly, a nonrepresentative board may result in a loss of constituents. On the other hand, a self-perpetuating board is very efficient, more predictable, and requires less staff attention than a membership-elected board. A self-perpetuating board offers management advantages such as day-to-day dealing with the board alone rather than spending time on the politics of board member elections. Deciding on the appropriate type of board structure is an important philosophical decision. Designing a new board can unify the board members into one governing body so that they no longer think in terms of "us against them" (McLaughlin, 1996, p. 15). Additionally, determining if voting privileges are essential to your members' sense of ownership, or if they would be committed members regardless of their ability to vote, is a matter of importance.

Designing the new board of directors, according to McLaughlin, is "an excellent opportunity to accomplish goals as diverse as rejuvenating the mission, streamlining board operations, and symbolizing the newly developed shared values of the merged organization. The governance structure is the major way of knitting together often-divergent participant goals and operational philosophies. Many considerations play into board structure, such as the board's optimal size and composition, terms of service, committee assignments, and the selection of board officers" (p. 14).

No hard and fast rules apply when assembling your board of directors. Rather, you will want to keep in mind your new organization's governance needs and organizational style and let those issues shape your decisions. The issues of board structure, size, and composition are much too large a subject to discuss at this writing. Remember that if you are changing your organization from a membership that elects the board to a board that elects itself (or vice versa), you may be faced with a whole array of political and infrastructure issues to secure the necessary votes required to effect this change.

From the perspective of trying to complete a merger, the important thing is not to let an initial posture on governance by one or more participants stifle discussion of the search for creative options. In looking for an appropriate model, it is best to look first for a basis that is defendable. Rather than measure one model against another, look for a practical board structure that can be defended to the directors and members. It is reasonable to assume that a particular governance model/board structure might be questioned. A model that is purely politically based may be hard to defend or explain. For example, if the model presented suggests that a majority of new board members are from organization A just because that is believed to be the only way to complete the merger, members of organizations B and C may not find the model palatable. It is usually beneficial to have several explanations for why one model is preferable over another. This justification has less of an impact when looking at models that provide for equitable representation for all parties. When balanced representation is not attainable, then defendable reasons for selecting an unbalanced representational board can mean the difference between having an organization accept the plan of merger or reject it.

Several considerations regarding governance modeling are presented below.

Geography

In this era of high technology, overnight mail, video conferencing, and the Internet, geography is not the issue it once was. However, if the nature of one or more of the merging organizations is such that a "high touch" approach is necessary to maintain local visibility or appropriate service to constituencies, then geography may be a factor in determining governance. Additionally, if the new board of directors will require a significant number of face-to-face meetings, geography is a governance factor because it affects meeting time and budgets. Last, if the organization is structured so that the top administration needs a significant amount of personal access to volunteer leadership, then geography is a governance issue.

Finances

Relative financial size frequently is used to determine governance models. There are many ways to look at finance, such as net vs. gross, total budget, and per capita income. For example, in one merger a nonprofit organization with a budget of $8 million merged with seven others, one with a $1.5 million budget and six with budgets below $1 million. The resultant board of directors included eight members from the large entity, two from the $1.5 million entity, and one each from the other six. The large entity had, in effect, a block vote. It certainly could significantly affect the direction of the corporation more easily.

Population

The size of one organization's constituency is another governance factor, especially in organizations that represent a geographically based constituency. Determining whether population is based on census data or number of organization members is relatively simple. The entities can present population data from a variety of governmental sources or provide a real number to their members. If the number of board members is based on population, you will need to select a method of determining the numbers and establish a specific periodic review to maintain the desired parity. Some organizations use census data. Others might use county birth rate. Deciding which data source to use may to some degree depend on the type of organization, because as the population grows, you could wind up with a very large board of directors. Adopting bylaws language forcing periodic review of any population-based governance model is imperative.

Variations on the population-based model also can work. For example, some governance models reflect the U.S. government House of Representatives (population based) and Senate (equal-participant based) concept. Additionally, voting can be scaled. For example, one director could have two votes and another could have .5 votes. On the surface this appears to be an inequitable model, but in certain circumstances such a structure can keep the board smaller while providing a more representative application of authority.

This is the time to look for compromise and to develop structure that is based on a condition that can be explained with integrity to interested parties. Also, consider the possibility of transitional governance models that will get the organization over some of the early resistance points.

Last, it is important to note that no governance model should be static and may and should be reconsidered periodically by the merged corporate board.

MERGING BYLAWS

In my experience, the merging of bylaws usually does not work effectively as a way to organize a new entity. First, bylaws have varying levels of sophistication. Second, bylaws sometimes reflect political or emotional postures that were present at the time they were drafted or amended. Third, if the organization has been around awhile, amendments to bylaws may have reduced the effectiveness of the original document. The bylaws of an older organization could tend to shape the new organization in its image and former culture. Additionally, bylaws are designed to provide internal governance and guidance. A new organization will need new bylaws if it is to be truly new. What is needed is a new organization governed by new rules, focused on a new future.

In recent years the trend of bylaws is to be flexible to some degree, while still providing direction on recurring issues, such as elections, director qualifications, and officers. Using bylaws as legislation rather than guidance rarely works to the advantage of the organization. Bylaws cluttered with "cannot dos" rather than "how to dos" are usually limiting, thus promoting future bylaws fights. Crafting bylaws language to protect a particular class or party to a merger, rather than to guide the new organization within the spirit of the merging environment, is counterproductive. Exhibit 4–2 provides a list of things to look for in a new organization's bylaws.

Most organizations have members or directors who make bylaws a priority. Having these people involved early is usually a good idea if any workgroup on governance is established. However, this group should be interspersed with people who understand how to maximize the purpose of bylaws and who are flexible in their approach to the document's preparation. Bylaws are intended to govern the welfare of the organization as a

Exhibit 4–2 Points To Check in Bylaws

Governance structure spelled out clearly

Nominations process carefully explained

Election procedure well defined

Voting requirements to amend clearly articulated

Current language regarding volunteer and director liability

Conforms to state law regarding meetings, rights of members, and other
   provisions

Does not violate any IRS code that could impact tax exemption

Does not define ad hoc committee structure

Does not reference employee contracts

Matches Articles of Incorporation where referenced

---

whole and not just address the issues of a few members. Also, bylaws are
not meant to address every eventuality; that is one reason to have a board
of directors to provide guidance and direction.

MAKING THE STRUCTURE WORK

The most important thing a carefully designed governance model
must do is make the organizational structure work. In nonprofit organizations, the structure must work in three ways. First, it must work inside out.
By that, I mean that governance must be responsive to the needs of its
constituency. These needs are defined in the "macro" context by the mission and in the "micro" context by constituency service. When structure
functions from the inside out, there is a perception by members and constituents that their elected or appointed volunteer board members are ful-

filling their responsibility by looking out for the best interest of the mission, the organization, and the constituency. Any organization whose board is perceived by a critical mass as not acting in the best interest of the mission is in trouble. Boards must be informed and must communicate a confident knowledge of the health and condition of the organization at all times. When a board appears to the primary constituency to be out of the loop, the structure is not working inside out. It is working "inside in," a sign of membership isolation that forebodes rocky times ahead.

Second, the governance structure also must work from the outside in. If your primary constituency feels isolated or perceives that the organization is no longer responsive to its needs and perception of the mission, it will take its support, volunteering, and donations elsewhere. Erosion of volunteer and membership support is bad enough, considering the cost of procurement, but to incur that loss because of a perception that a volunteer has no access to participate is even more costly. Volunteers and members must be able to see a clear track to leadership for an organization to realize real health. Even if the organization has a nonrepresentative, self-perpetuating board of directors, there needs to be a system of volunteer leadership cultivation that prevents the board from appearing to be an elitist club that does not welcome the input of others. Ensuring that a board is open to its constituency and provides access for its members is critical to making an outside-in structure work and is imperative for organizational success.

Third, governance must work from the top down. With all due respect to recent "bottom-up" organizational theory, the truth is that most nonprofit organizations work because they are primarily staff driven. Staff at some level carries out the vision and strategic work of the board. Therefore, any governance model that does not support and empower senior staff will place excess responsibility on the board, resulting in volunteer burnout and, eventually, lost effectiveness of the organization. The biggest myth in the entire nonprofit world is that volunteers drive organizations. While volunteers provide work, fuel, money, vision, energy, emotion, passion, and direction, staff drives operations. Operations is the infrastructure that supports the mission.

REFERENCES

McLaughlin, T. A. (1996). *Seven steps to a successful nonprofit merger*. Washington, DC: National Center for Nonprofit Boards.

CHAPTER 5

Dissolution vs. Merger

T HE NOTION OF BECOMING a different corporation seems to be hard for some nonprofit organizations (NPOs) to grasp. That is why merger is frequently referred to as a marriage between two corporations. In effect, one or more accepts the change of name of another and pledges all of its holdings, assets, debts, personnel, and everything else to the other corporation. This notion is palatable because all parties of the marriage expect to get something out of the event.

The expectation of who gets what is the hard part. That is why the negotiations discussed in a previous chapter are so important. The negotiations result in two documents (discussed fully in the next chapter): bylaws and a plan and agreement to merge. These documents, to continue with our metaphor on marriage, in essence become the prenuptial agreement. It is in these documents that all the concerns are addressed, the conditions and expectations of all parties are recorded, and how the major issues of the merger will be handled post-merger is spelled out.

This negotiation process in the early days will focus on the issues presented in Chapter 4. Once the parties have agreed to proceed with merger and have resolved the governance, leadership, and structural organization issues, the particulars of the merger really begin.

While this chapter has been reviewed by legal counsel, it should be noted that the information presented is not to be considered legal advice. Legal advice should be obtained only from a lawyer authorized to practice law.

This chapter focuses on true mergers, in which two or more corporate entities meld into a surviving entity. The term "surviving entity" means that when a merger occurs, one organization appears to go away and everything attached to it becomes part of the surviving entity. The surviving corporation carries on the business formerly conducted by the other merging corporations. With this in mind, some important technical decisions must be made when making the decision to merge. You will need expert legal help in this phase of the merger. Additionally, the technical process should rest with one responsible party. Your consultant should fill the role of coordinating the legal team so all technical details are collected in one place.

DISSOLUTION VS. MERGER AND CONTROL OF ASSETS

Early in the merger negotiations, the legal issues should be identified and reviewed. These issues may involve "political concerns (such as neither organization wanting to 'disappear'), legal concerns (such as the vagaries of state laws on non-profit organizations), and tax concerns" (Greif, 1990, p. 34). When some people think about merging companies, their first reaction is to assume one organization is dissolving and one is surviving. It's not uncommon to hear people talk about one corporation dissolving when they really mean that a merger has occurred. It is important for anyone considering merger to understand the difference between merging two organizations and dissolving one corporation and moving its assets to another corporation. The latter is a much more complex procedure.

First of all, dissolution of a nonprofit entity is controlled to some extent by the language in its articles of incorporation, or bylaws, regarding dissolution. The language in those documents often states that upon dissolution of the corporation, its assets are to be turned over to some other tax-exempt entity. Other organizations may have delegated a court of appropriate jurisdiction to distribute their assets upon dissolution. This type of language may not allow for the joining of assets contemplated in a merger through dissolution. Because of the complexity of these issues, dissolving one corporation and moving its assets to another is usually not the best path to choose.

Dissolution of an organization may also require that you know every detail of all the organization's assets, where those assets are, and who holds the title. An organization may end up with a forgotten asset or one that it did not know existed being lost forever in dissolution. Additionally, dissolution means an organization physically no longer exists in any form. In a merger, an organization's identity is merged or converted into an existing or new organization. For example, if a supporter in the outer regions of your service area cared about your organization and mentioned your organization by name in his or her will, and your corporate entity dissolves before the will is probated, then you may lose the gift. However, if your organization merges with another organization, and it appears as if your organization became another corporation, the merged organization will usually get the gift because most states have survivor rights, which allow the monies or assets from a will or estate to be shifted into the newly merged corporation.

Here's another example of how the transfer of property works in merger. Let's say that Corporation A owns a van. The van is registered to Corporation A, and a license plate check shows Corporation A as the owner. If Corporation A merges with Corporation B, which becomes the survivor corporation, upon filing of appropriate documents, and a usually brief period for the filings to be recognized by the respective states, then a check on the license plate of the van would indicate that it belongs to

Corporation B. This transfer of ownership occurs even if Corporation B is in a different state. In this case, Corporation A's asset became an asset of Corporation B.

DETERMINING THE SURVIVING ORGANIZATION

Usually one of the first negotiation issues revolves around starting a new corporation and merging all entities into that one, or selecting one of the corporate structures to survive.

In most nonprofit mergers, one organization survives and the others no longer separately exist even though their assets and physical property continue under new ownership and governance. Sometimes the issue of survivorship is a sensitive political challenge. A consultant or legal counsel is usually the preferred party to resolve this issue on behalf of all participants. Developing a creative name for the newly merged entity can sometimes solve the issue. In extreme cases, a brand-new entity can be developed and all the parties merged into it. Note that this solution is more expensive, takes much more time, and multiplies the layers of paperwork, not the least of which could be achieving recognition for the new entity as a tax-exempt organization. Merging all parties into one new corporation (not typical in nonprofit mergers) may result in a myriad of tax and fundraising problems; it generally is not advisable.

Size and Revenue

A number of factors come into play when you begin to consider the question of which will be the survivor organization in a merger. These involve discovering which organization possesses the most assets in capital and revenue because this organization might serve as the best choice for the core of the new operation. Given equal consideration of all other factors, the entity with the larger number of hard assets will more easily absorb the assets and operations of the smaller entity when forming a new, larger organization.

Another consideration is liabilities. It may be advisable for the organization with large liabilities or past credit problems to merge into a new organization with a new name not to avoid debt—the liabilities will follow the merger—but to reduce public recognition of past problems.

State Laws and Statutes

Another factor to consider when deciding which entity to select as the survivor concerns the nonprofit laws and statutes in the home state(s) of each merging organization. These statutes need to be looked at from two or three different perspectives. The first of these is: how current are these statutes? In some states, changes have been going on in nonprofit statutes since the mid-1970s, but other states have been slower to adopt modern codes. The state statutes that reflect modern changes and are more nonprofit friendly should be favored.

Some states are more accommodating to nonprofit organizations than other states. For example, some states do not provide nonprofits with tax relief on buildings they own and occupy. However, choosing a survivor organization in a nonprofit-friendly state may not provide all the relief you are seeking if your operation and or principal offices are in another state. Your legal counsel can help with this decision.

The Corporate Name

Yet another issue in determining survivorship is the desirability of retaining a certain corporate name. Some states are careful about the use of corporate names that may confuse the public. A new corporation may have difficulty achieving the exact name it wishes. Most states have a procedure of checking the availability of a corporate name and reserving a particular name if it is available. It is possible that a corporation may have a name that is allowed in one state but not in another. If your merger will result in a company that will operate across state lines, the availability of names should be checked in all states before a survivor corporation is determined.

Experience shows that volunteers and leaders of NPOs are not keen on the constant changing of decisions they believe have been made. For example, if a CEO tells his or her board of directors that their corporation will be the survivor and they will keep their name and later finds out that is not possible because of the conditions mentioned in the previous paragraph, volunteers tend to question the permanence of other decisions as well.

FUNDRAISING REGULATIONS

Others factors that need to be examined within nonprofit codes are the state regulations on fundraising. Some states require nonprofit organizations to register and report their fundraising activities to the state. Additionally, some states charge significant fees for registering nonprofit organizations. Other states place limits on the amount of annual fundraising that any particular nonprofit is allowed. This means that placing the newly merged organization's headquarters in that state can potentially restrict the operational aspects of that organization. To conclude that a state is nonprofit friendly is to look at all of these factors and make a determination.

The whole issue of fundraising requires significant study. Fundraising is the lifeblood of NPOs, and any loss of fundraising success or market share can have a catastrophic impact on an organization. In timing a merger, consideration should be made as to where an organization is in its fundraising cycle. The merger will drain staff time. Staff committed to fundraising could be required to work on the merger and lose valuable resource production time. Plan for a loss or flat funding cycle during merger talks and merger voting, and in the time immediately after the merger.

In addition, some states have restrictions against certain types of fundraising activities. If one or more of those activities are critical to your financial success, you will need to factor the impact of that potential loss in your merger evaluation equation and also the state of record and survivorship.

VOLUNTEER AND MEETING CONSIDERATIONS

Another component in the survivorship decision is in the flexibility of holding meetings. Some states do not allow nonprofit, or even for-profit, entities to meet electronically. This can be very inconvenient for those organizational leaders who need the flexibility of meeting through conference telephone calls. Meetings using fax machines or other electronic means are currently not provided for in most state statutes. In most cases, at a minimum, the participants must be able to hear and be heard. As an example, hearing and being heard would prevent a meeting from being held in a chat room over the Internet.

VOLUNTEER LIABILITY PROTECTION

The Volunteer Protection Act of 1997 (Pub. L. No. 105 – 19) limits the liability of all nonpaid volunteers and directors. This act may be enhanced with greater protection by state law, but because the federal act is inclusive, picking a state based purely on volunteer protection is no longer an issue. The whole notion of volunteer liability, however, is.

Many volunteers are concerned that decisions made regarding a merger may cause them some form of personal liability. Such liability problems are rare. If your volunteers are concerned about liability, you should have a competent legal authority answer this question. Liability for a volunteer participating in a merger decision normally would result only if there was evidence of fraud or misrepresentation. Such a misrepresentation that resulted in personal gain might become a litigious situation for the volunteer.

In any case, reviewing the state law to determine volunteer liability protection in the survivor state is advisable.

REFERENCES

Greif, J. (1990, Summer). Association mergers: Tax and other planning. *The Journal of Taxation of Exempt Organizations*, 32–35.

CHAPTER 6

Technical and Legal Aspects

W HILE THIS SECTION of this book has been reviewed by legal counsel, it should be noted that the information presented is not to be considered legal advice. Legal advice should be obtained only from a lawyer authorized to practice law.

Once the surviving organization is selected, the process of beginning the merger starts with the thorough examination of the state statutes that govern mergers in the states that are involved. Virtually all states have a specific code that identifies the steps to follow to ensure that the merger is completed legally. Additionally, your investigation needs to include detailed research of the articles of incorporation and bylaws that govern the individual merging organizations. Many times state statutes defer to the specifications of an organization's articles of incorporation or bylaws, and these documents will govern how the voting, and other aspects of the merger, must be completed. If the state statutes are silent on certain key issues, and the bylaws speak to these issues, it is customary to defer to the bylaws. A topic such as the amount of advance notice that must be given to organization members when informing them of merger voting is an example of the type of information you will need. In some cases, state statues are very specific on the merger process and may supersede bylaws. The key is to remember that you can't assume that the way you've normally conducted business will legally suffice during the merger process. Complete and thorough research of the state's nonprofit codes regarding mergers needs to be a central part of your decision-making processes, and you will need legal counsel and expert consulting guidance on all technical issues. This research will also result in an indication of how to time the merger process (a section showing a typical timeline is presented in Chapter 4).

VOTING APPROVAL

Along with the regulations dictating the minimal amount of advance notice you need to give your board of directors and members concerning merger meetings, you also must be clear about the voting approval requirements. Your bylaws may have allowed you to handle all organizational decisions with a majority vote of the board of directors. However, you may find that to fulfill state statutes that govern a merger, you are required to have a two-thirds approval vote of all members. To meet such a requirement, identifying who your members are, from a legal perspective, is a critical issue. It is vital to remember that depending on how state statutes are written, you may have to conform to them even if they are different from your bylaws and normal operating procedures. Otherwise, the merger might be judged invalid. Therefore, coordinating the legal issues surrounding the merger is a critical element of any merger process.

STAYING ORGANIZED

To help your understanding of the requirements of the state codes, create a chart that shows specifically the tasks that need to be completed and whose responsibility they are. As you research, you may discover that if your membership has the authority to elect your board of directors, you have to subscribe to one set of rules, while if your board of directors is self-perpetuating, you need to subscribe to only a portion of these rules, or to a different set of rules, when voting on the merger. You also will discover how much advance notice you must give the board of directors and members before a merger vote is taken. This required notice could be as little as five days or up to more than 60 days. Usually it falls between 20 and 30 days. In some cases, the state laws defer to the bylaws. In some cases, bylaws are silent on this issue. When this occurs, you should always use your state's suggested notice requirements. See Appendix B for an example of the different voting and notification requirements the American Cancer Society had to meet for a single merger.

When bylaws and the state statutes are not in agreement, follow the guidelines that allow for the longer period of time, if at all possible. This way, the members of your organization will be less likely to feel the merger is proceeding in a manner that does not conform to past practices. Also, they will have less ammunition to contest the vote if they are so inclined. Creating a calendar to keep abreast of all critical dates so mailings and notices will not be missed is a good idea.

NONBINDING VOTES

These technical requirements discussed in this chapter concern only the meetings in which voting on the merger will take place. The discussion phase surrounding the decision to merge should be completed before these voting meetings (see Chapter 3). Even if your discussion meetings have ended with the board of directors accepting a nonbinding resolution to consider, or accept, the merger, the legal merger procedure doesn't start until you send an official notice saying that you are going to contemplate merger and vote on it. Any informal votes or favorable discussions held before the official meetings are not usually legally binding—the actual merger process begins when you send the correct documents to your voting members at the appropriate time.

NOTIFYING VOTING MEMBERS

After you have determined the lead time required for mailing out the notice for the merger vote, you must determine what attachments and inclusions to send with the notice. Sometimes, state statutes are very specific as to what must be included. In addition to the obvious information, such as, time, date, and location of the meeting, some state statutes require specific language be present in the notice (see Appendix C for a sample notice). State law usually requires inclusion of the agreement or plan of merger or a summary of its terms. Additional items that should generally be enclosed in the notice include prepared bylaws of the new organization, articles of merger, and the resolution to merge that the members will be asked to adopt. In some states, articles of merger are referred to as a certificate of merger.

Additionally, it is vital to ensure that everybody who has a vote on the matter is provided proper notice. If someone who was entitled to notice was not notified or did not have the complete information, he or she could potentially block the merger with legal action. Of course, such action not only would delay the merger but could be publicly and politically embarrassing to the organizations.

State laws require that mergers be effective pursuant to an agreement of merger or a plan of merger. It is customary to structure the merger document as a "plan and agreement" to accommodate defining requirements among the states involved. The negotiation of the various aspects of the merger occurs before the drafting of the plan and agreement to merge. It is this document that forms the framework of the merger and reflects the understanding of what the postmerger entity will look like. See Appendix D for an example of a plan and agreement to merge.

The plan and agreement to merge is the first document to be agreed upon after the boards of directors hold their preliminary discussions concerning merging. Before you register any votes, it is vital that the two merging entities have met, discussed, and agreed upon all components of the merger. Once the plan and agreement is submitted for a vote, it is no longer a negotiation item and parties may not change it unilaterally. Additionally, bylaws are frequently referred to in agreements to merge because they reflect the governance model, and parties may not unilaterally change them. The major decisions made earlier, including the decision on the state of survivorship, will provide the basis for the plan and agreement to merge. The governance structure of the new organization, bylaws, and the list of those who will compose its initial board of directors also may be part of the plan and agreement.

Most of these overarching decisions mentioned above will be listed and spelled out specifically in the plan and agreement to merge. However, some of these decisions, such as those concerning governance, should be included in companion documents such as the bylaws of the newly merged corporation or a specific memorandum of understanding that may form a contractual basis for some expected future action. If this is the case, the bylaws and any other accompanying documents should be attached to the summary of the plan and agreement to merge that is sent to all those within the merging organizations with authority to vote. The advantage of including provisions in the bylaws is that they can subsequently be modified by amendment. Provisions included in the plan and agreement to merge and the resultant plan of merger may not be amendable after the merger has become effective.

To clarify the process further, the board of directors or members will adopt a "resolution to merge." This resolution authorizes the formal adoption of the plan and agreement to merge and should be constructed to satisfy the legal merger process for each party pursuant to applicable law (see Appendix E for a sample resolution to merge). The plan and agreement to merge is then drafted and may refer to the newly agreed upon bylaws, which protect governance and other documents that may be attached to protect or clarify other concerns. The "articles of merger" or "certificate of merger" is the final document that is filed with state governments to make the merger official (see Appendix F). Exhibit 6–1 shows the flow of the merger process.

Exhibit 6-1 Negotiating and Finding Agreement

---

1. Negotiate and find agreement on governance and other issues.

2. Draft or redraft BYLAWS to bring the new entity in line with contemporary code requirements, remove superfluous references, and cast the internal governance model of the new organization post-merger.

3. Draft a PLAN AND AGREEMENT TO MERGE clarifying how/who votes/when they vote and referencing the bylaws and other major considerations.

4. All parties independently adopt a RESOLUTION TO MERGE before the merger becomes effective according to the notice and vote requirements spelled out in the Plan and Agreement to Merge.

5. Draft and file ARTICLES OF MERGER or CERTIFICATE OF MERGER, and any other legal documents indicating the plan is accepted by all parties (usually with accompanying notarized signatures of appropriate officers of all parties).

CHOOSING THE DATE OF THE MERGER

Try to choose a date for the merger to go into effect that falls at the end of a typical accounting period, such as the end of a fiscal year, a calendar year, or an accounting quarter. If the merging organizations do not share a common accounting calendar, it is wise to choose a date that coincides with the end of a reporting period for the entity that is not the survivor. This will assist in auditing and probably be less expensive.

Always check state laws. A few do not authorize the selection of an effective date and will require that the merger documents actually be filed on (or as close as possible to) the desired effective date. Selecting an effective date that occurs prior to the filing date is not permitted by any state. In some states, such as New York, the effective date of the merger is determined by the courts upon their review of the articles of merger.

MAKING THE VOTE LEGAL

Once the resolution, summary, plan of agreement to merge, and by-laws are sent to the board of directors with proper notification, the board is permitted to vote. If there is a question regarding the vote passing successfully according to the state statutes or according to the bylaws, you must heed the regulations in the state statutes to avoid the validity of the merger being successfully challenged in the future. If your organization does not have members or another body that is authorized to elect your directors, in most states the merger process is completed with the board's vote. Some states require a board of directors to vote two times at two separate meetings with different levels of affirmative votes required for passage each time (Kansas is an example). Check the laws in your state regarding this process.

If there is a membership, and your organizational documents do not specifically provide your directors with the authority to merge without membership approval, you still have work to do. Once the board of directors has passed the resolution to merge, the entire process of notification, meeting, and voting must begin all over again with your membership. Voting requirements and notice may (and generally will) be different for the membership. In most states, the process is designed to be sequential: board notice – board vote – member notice – member vote.

Once the vote to merge is passed by the board of directors and members, you have reached the end of the voting component of the legal process. It is necessary to file the signed articles or certificate of merger and any other ancillary documents required by your state with secretaries of state and state departments of corporation and/or commerce by the effective date. Some states require other filings with counties in which the corporation has property. Some states require notice of the merger to be published in a local newspaper or newspaper of legal record. Check state laws. On the selected effective date, the merger is then official. A few states do not authorize selection of an effective date other than the filing date. See "Choosing the date of the merger" above for details.

THE VOTING MEETING

Meetings to vote on mergers typically fall into two categories. The first category is the easiest to handle. The leadership of the organization or your consultant explains the plan and agreement to merge, announces that the merger committee, or the board of directors, is recommending that the plan be approved, and asks for a motion for vote on the merger. No specific type of vote is generally required—if your organization normally accepts a voice vote or a show of hands, then either type of vote is acceptable as long as no voters protest. If a voter protests, the group should be polled (upon proper motion) as to how the members wish to proceed. At this point, an individual makes a motion to vote. In some cases, there might be very little discussion, the organization votes, and the merger is complete. The secretary or assistant secretary of the corporation usually certifies the vote. If your bylaws and state statutes allow proxies, you may vote by proxy.

Often, a number of questions arise because the board of directors or members have failed to review all the materials associated with the entire merger discussion. Having a consultant present at these meetings is vital, as the consultant often has been involved throughout each part of the process and can usually respond to questions. The consultant becomes the point person to answer the majority of questions. This technique also serves to take the attention off key staff and volunteer leadership. Reducing the target profile of those who will remain with the organization is a wise tactic. Also, the consultant, being external to the organization, can respond to emotionally based questions and issues in a more clinical fashion.

It also is important to keep in mind that with more than one entity voting on the same set of documents, one group cannot unilaterally alter documents that were previously agreed upon by other parties. If this were allowed, there would have to be multiple meetings with numerous votes to reach agreement. Further, such action would diminish the value of the efforts of the negotiating team. In situations involving individuals who raise questions that might involve a potential change in the documents, the consultant should reassure them that their concerns will be considered at one of the first meetings of the new board of directors. Once this assurance is given, make sure there is follow-up with those who had concerns regarding the board's response to their issues.

However, you also may approve a document conditionally, stipulating that modification of certain identified points in the future will invalidate the vote. Likewise, you can stipulate specific circumstances that must occur before the vote of your group will be valid. Your leadership team can then approach the other leadership team and explain that its group approved the merger, but with conditions. Working out a compromise between leaders in this manner allows for due diligence while allowing the vote to proceed expeditiously. Usually, it is advisable to draft resolutions in such a way as to authorize the officers of the corporation to make minor or specified changes to the documents without a new vote.

The most challenging aspect of managing a voting meeting is trying to create an atmosphere in which each merging organization, even if it is the surviving one, does not feel as if it is dying or voting itself out of business. Another important component is to allow members and directors, who often feel disenfranchised by the merger, to continue their involvement in the newly formed organization in a meaningful way. The vote to merge will often mean a large number of board members will raise their hands to support the merger, and, in doing so, give up their voice and/or director's responsibility in an organization that has great meaning for them. Acknowledge this, and address the involvement needs of your volunteers, staff, and supporters at the earliest phases of the merger process. There are several good ways to continue meaningful volunteer connection to the organization. It can start with a celebration event shortly after the merger is completed. These celebration events can be held jointly or just with the old boards. I have a preference for holding them together as a launch to the "new world order" when practical and appropriate.

Another connection method is to use the former volunteers on special committees of the board and appoint them to task forces and workgroups. Still another technique is to establish some type of honorary group to which former leaders can be elected that will provide them with an appropriate level of thanks and keep them attached.

Send former board members meeting agendas and information about upcoming events as a means of easing them out of their post. Inviting them to functions is also an effective relationship management tool.

ELECTING A NEW BOARD OF DIRECTORS

In some cases, the merger documents may specify how to elect a new board of directors. Generally, premerger discussions on governance will specify a method of determining the initial board of directors. If there is no other method determined and the newly merged entity is a directorship corporation, the individual merging governing boards may elect the initial new board. In preparation for this vote, a nominating committee, or similar process, should submit a list of names to be considered for the new board along with their terms of office. The nominations may be voted upon at the meeting at which the final merger vote is taken. Alternatively, the merger documents may include the names and terms of the new directors, allowing a single vote of the participating boards to pass both issues. If the new entity is a membership corporation in which a group of members are empowered to elect the board of directors, or trustees, then an election procedure must be established and followed according to bylaws and, in some cases, prescribed state statutes. In these cases, the merger documents sometimes name an interim board of directors to remain in office until such a formal election can be held.

Another way to approach the selection of a new board of directors, assuming the new entity is organized on a directorship basis, is to allow the merging organization representatives to choose the representatives to the new board. Upon creating the new entity, those board members are subject to the bylaws of the merged organization, thereby dissolving any further divisions between the members. A third option for a membership corporation would allow the merging organizations to create classes of members to make ongoing decisions about their board representation even after they have become a single entity.

OTHER LEGAL ISSUES

Organizations must consider numerous other issues such as the ramifications of merging employee benefit plans, vacation policies, sick leave, and more. Adopting and filing the appropriate resolutions is necessary if either organization has an employee benefit plan concerning retirement funds and insurance that binds the corporation (see Appendix G). Employee issues are more complicated when they involve employees of an entity in one state that merges into an entity organized under the laws of another state. Additionally, the Internal Revenue Service needs to be notified that one organization has merged into another in order to get appropriate tax exemption carried forward without a break in coverage.

A review is essential for any pending litigation to determine its effect on a merging organization. Merger of an organization that is under litigation or threat of legal action usually means that the action will transfer to the new entity. Check directors' and officers' liability insurance and other insurance policies to ensure there will be no time gap in coverage.

A thorough due diligence review of leases and contracts should be undertaken for provisions relating to mergers. Banks or other lenders may have the capacity to call a loan or mortgage due upon merger of the corporation. These issues can usually be worked out, but if they are not resolved before the merger becomes effective the organization may find itself in default. See Appendix H for examples of other banking documents that are often part of a merger. The terms of specific bequests should also be reviewed because sometimes they contain surprising restrictions on the merging entities, with contingent beneficiaries who stand to gain if you violate the restrictions.

In one case, a charity in Oklahoma was named in the estate of a donor for a large gift. The entity was merging with three other corporations, and the survivor was to be in Missouri. Upon review of the estate bequest, it was noted that the corporation receiving the bequest was required to be a corporation organized under the laws of Oklahoma. In this case, the merging entities agreed to maintain a separate corporation in Oklahoma with overlapping directorates until the planned gift was realized.

The charity could have reentered into discussions with the donor's estate executors to change the content of the specific state requirement. But because the gift was worth several million dollars, the corporation elected the method described above rather than risk the loss of the bequest.

CREATING A DOCUMENT-TRACKING NOTEBOOK

It is strongly recommend that any organization working on a merger create a notebook with all the documents required to complete the merger. My experience indicates that organizing the documents in chronological order is the most efficient method (see Appendix I for a list of documents frequently required in mergers). This notebook would contain the following items:

- A copy of the board's intent to merge resolution

- A copy of the notice that was sent to the board of directors of the meeting where a vote was taken to merge

- A copy of the resolution(s) to merge and all other relevant resolutions

- A copy of the plan and agreement to merge

- A copy of the signed articles of merger with signatures of all parties

- All Certificates of Authority to do business in other states, if necessary (see Appendix J)

- A copy of the legal newspaper notice announcing the merger, if required

- A copy of the attorney general or court action permitting merger, if required (e.g., in states such as Vermont, Tennessee, and New York)

- Any other pertinent documents such as evidence of filing

- The minutes of the meetings signed by the secretary of the organization in which the agreements to merge were adopted, showing that there was a quorum present, that a vote was taken, and the results of the vote (see Appendix K)

- Any amendments to articles of incorporation

- Any new amendments or restatement of bylaws

Four or five copies of this notebook should be prepared. One remains with the surviving organization office of the CEO, another with the CFO, and one goes to legal counsel. The spare copy or two are sure to come in handy.

CHAPTER 7

Working with Consultants and Attorneys

HIRING A CONSULTANT

MANY ORGANIZATIONS FIND that a nonpartisan consultant can provide indispensable help throughout the merger process. First, he or she can help you understand what merger means and what to expect during the process. Second, a consultant can help you design a model, including structural and operational scenarios, of the resulting merged organization. Keep in mind that consultants are hired "to help all involved make the best decisions for their respective organizations in as short a time as possible" (La Piana, 1995, p. 3).

A consultant also can help you overcome the emotional and political barriers that might hinder your early thinking. Because a consultant is distanced from your commitment to your mission, he or she can help you accurately assess whether you are a viable merger candidate and can evaluate your relative negotiation strength. Some organizations use their consultant as an ambassador—a third-party representative who can determine if one or more entities are interested in merging and, if so, under what conditions.

Make sure your consultant has experience in merging tax-exempt organizations (Lewis and Chandler, 1993, p. 90). An experienced consultant will be able to outline the technical process of your merger and help you develop an organizational political strategy. Your consultant should be able to provide several initial governance models and bylaws language to help protect all parties. Greif (1990) suggests that the consultant should be brought on board very early in the merger process, and his or her fees should be shared equally among the organizations involved. Finally, a consultant can become the buffer between organizations to prevent irreparable relationship damage among volunteers, staff, leadership, and other constituencies. Thomas A. McLaughlin (1996) believes a consultant is important because an "independent consultant may facilitate the process in order to ensure that the focus remains on the problem at hand rather than the people working on the problem" (p. 9).

Not many organizational consultants have extensive experience in nonprofit mergers. The first step in finding a consultant should be placing a call to organizations that you know have experienced a merger and asking about their consulting team. An Internet search also might produce a consultant to interview. Be wary of individuals who say they can facilitate mergers but have little or no actual experience. It is also advisable to avoid merger consultants whose proposals focus more on traditional organizational support, such as strategic planning, mission development, and goal setting, rather than the tactical structural and technical help related to mergers.

Developing a Tactical Plan

Developing a strong tactical plan before a merger is critical. Tactical planning is a linear process. It progresses through various steps of the plan and ends, hopefully, with the desired results. The components of a tactical merger plan can be categorized into two areas: philosophical and operational.

The tactical philosophy is important because it provides volunteer and staff leaders with the direction needed to develop the more linear operational tactics. Tactical philosophy can take many forms and even combine forms when appropriate. For example, an overarching tactical philosophy could be that you want the entire negotiations process to be completed before notifying mid-level staff or volunteers. Another philosophy is to have open communications between senior management and all staff from the beginning. There is a saying in merger deliberations that "ambiguity is your friend." This refers to the concept of not being excessively clear on some or all of the merger facts. The thinking in this is that the more specific details of how the merger will actually be formed may give detractors more fuel for the fire.

Another reason to be less specific about exactly how the merger may be formed is to avoid employee flight. This issue is even more important when the labor market is tight.

If the tactical philosophy is to be more open, then the communications down to the lowest levels of the organization must be early, consistent, and often. E-mail and websites are excellent tools for dissemination of accurate information.

Cost of Consultants

The cost of consultants can vary depending on the services you need and the size and scope of the merger. The more legal jurisdictions (or states) involved, the greater the cost. Fees can vary from a few thousand dollars for a simple two-unit, single-state merger to more than $100,000 for large multistate, multicompany mergers.

Unless you are a tax-exempt specialist with a background in nonprofit corporate law, you should seriously consider using a consultant. Using a consultant as your staff point person will free chief administrators to focus their energies on planning, political issues, and securing the necessary votes.

A consultant can also be helpful in keeping the senior staff protected somewhat from potential volunteer backlash. That is, volunteers who do not favor a merger can vent their disagreement toward the consultant and not directly at an executive director or other senior staff members.

A key role of a knowledgeable consultant includes two other important areas. First, the consultant will keep the process on task and on time. He or she does not have to worry about the day-to-day activities of the organizations in the merger process. Second, an experienced consultant will be able to answer most of the questions you and your volunteers have about merger conditions, merger process, and the technical aspects of merger. This will keep the process moving on track rather than allowing it to stall while senior staff and volunteers find answers to their questions and concerns.

USING ATTORNEYS

The legal complexities of a merger will require that you get legal assistance. Although you are using an experienced consultant to guide the flow and tactics of the process, the technical nature of merger requires legal help.

First, try to find a lawyer with merger experience, specifically nonprofit experience. Not many firms have this expertise, but in the end, it will be less expensive and the results will probably be more to your expectation if you find such an experienced legal partner. Your consultant should be able to help you find and negotiate a price with a qualified lawyer.

Second, make sure your lawyer understands the sensitive nature of nonprofit mergers. Many attorneys will focus their efforts on the technical nature of merger and may not be helpful in working on the emotional aspects of nonprofit mergers that are germane due to the volunteer nature of the organizations. For example, one common merger technique is to start by creating a brand-new corporation with a new name and merging the other entities into the new entity. While this idea may be good for for-profit companies, in which the focus is on the negotiations regarding assets, it may not satisfy the cultural and historical need of a nonprofit organization (NPO). In addition, it may result in the loss of a planned gift, as discussed earlier. Make sure your attorney understands that the merger can fail on even the seemingly most insignificant point if volunteers get upset. In NPO mergers, there is no such thing as one person, one vote. The voting process is much more subtle. A judgment error by an attorney that certain points are insignificant, because they are insignificant from a legal perspective, can jeopardize the entire process.

WORKING WITH OTHER PROFESSIONALS AND VOLUNTEERS

Other professionals may be of assistance in merger deliberations and preparations. These include certified public accountants (CPAs) or your audit partners. The larger accounting firms have become adept at developing a relationship with their customers that transcends the traditional accountant role, and such a relationship can be of assistance in merger. Audit partners frequently know more about the economic condition of your organization than anyone besides your chief financial officer (CFO), if you have one. Smaller NPOs frequently do not have in-house financial expertise of the level needed to make good merger decisions based on finance.

As stated earlier in this book, NPO mergers are not based solely on financial concerns. Listen to the advice and counsel of your lawyer and CPA, and base your decisions on what you and your staff and volunteer leadership believe is best for the mission of the organization.

Keep in mind that you may have significant expertise within your volunteer ranks when it comes to mergers. Many large and small for-profit corporations have experienced mergers. An executive with such a company could benefit staff and make other volunteers more comfortable with the merger notion.

Other expertise to look for within your volunteer ranks includes tax and IRS specialists, banking professionals, and other financial and legal talent. Caution is advised regarding turning over the technical responsibility to one or more key volunteers for two main reasons. First, if the volunteer is providing some of the services on a pro bono basis, it will be difficult to ensure the process is being completed in a timely manner. Second, many of the professionals mentioned work on an hourly or purely professional basis without a specific fee determined at the start. If the volunteer elects to bill the NPO for services and the fee is not deemed fair, it may be difficult to negotiate an equitable settlement for all parties within the context of volunteer to volunteer.

For example, one NPO that was party to a merger elected to use a lawyer who was a member of its board of directors as its counsel. The merger was completed successfully, but the lawyer billed the NPO for more than $15,000 in fees. The other parties to the merger paid outside law firms $5,000 to $7,000 each. The work for each of the parties was similar. The NPO paid the higher fee, but there were hard feelings among the volunteers and the NPO leadership.

Using professionals is an important piece of the merger process. There are just too many details and pieces of technical information for an NPO executive and staff to keep up with while continuing to run the organization. Your consultant and others on your merger professional team will focus their attention on these details. You have only one chance to do the merger correctly. Finding the best-qualified consultants, lawyers, and others to assist in the process will be well worth your time and money at the end of the day.

REFERENCES

Greif, J. (1990, Summer). Association mergers: Tax and other planning. *The Journal of Taxation of Exempt Organizations*, 32–35.

La Piana, D. (1995). *Nonprofit mergers*. Washington, DC: National Center for Nonprofit Boards.

Lewis, F. C., & Chandler, C. R. (1993, March). The urge to merge: A common-sense approach to association consolidation. *Association Management*, 81–84.

McLaughlin, T. A. (1996). *Seven steps to a successful nonprofit merger*. Washington, DC: National Center for Nonprofit Boards.

CHAPTER 8

Transitioning To Merge

A S A MERGER CONSULTANT, I am frequently asked, "What happens on the first day of the merger?" In my experience the answer to this question is, "Very little." Most nonprofit organization mergers, because of the political sensitivity surrounding the emotional and organizational issues that often accompany major changes, do not experience immediate transformation in policy or operation. New boards usually empower the structure that existed pre-merger to operate "business as usual" until post-merger organization can begin. Of course, you may develop a completely merged organization to be effective on the date of merger. If you choose to do this, be prepared for a longer development time for the merger process. Depending upon size and structure of the organizations involved it could take 10 to 12 months of intensive preparation to have a merger completely functional on the merger date following your board's or members' final vote.

An additional barrier to completing a merger to full functionality at the chosen merger date is employee and staff unrest. If employees believe that on the merger date their jobs may be in jeopardy, there may be personnel flight from one or more of the corporations at a time when loss in productivity could have a major negative impact on your plans. Unless other factors indicate differently, nonprofit organizations should merge first and then begin reorganization. This is not to say there should be no planning regarding the potential structure, rather that implementation should be announced on the effective date of the merger or shortly thereafter. There are, however, some ways to smooth the transition to full merger.

One of the surprising things about mergers to most people is that, even after the effective date, merging operations is an evolving process, not an event. In all mergers, for-profit and nonprofit alike, it takes months (or even years) for complex entities to become one fully merged unit. In nonprofit mergers, several considerations must be addressed early on. In my experience, these issues can become less difficult to address by creating a "transition team."

The transition team usually consists of the top two levels of administrative staff from all merged parties. As a minimum, the team should include chief executive officers (CEOs), if appointed, chief operating officers (COOs), and chief financial officers (CFOs) of each merged organization. This group would then bring on board ad hoc team members consisting of other staff or volunteers as deemed appropriate to focus on arising issues and concerns.

Figure 8–1 demonstrates the transition team composition.

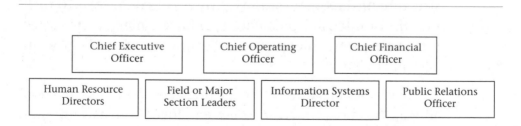

Figure 8–1 Transition Team

The transition team will need to meet regularly. The more issues there are to resolve, the more often they should meet. Once or twice weekly is not uncommon. If you have chosen an open communications model, step up the flow of information as soon as the transition team is formed. There are examples of actually developing a "rumor control" team consisting of highly respected and regarded employees from varying levels of the organization. This team receives regular briefings from one or more of the transition team members and is charged with getting essential information to all employees. These teams can be very helpful in preventing mass turnover of employees and do much to resolve the personal unrest that usually accompanies merger.

VOLUNTEER RELATIONS ISSUES

The newly merged organization will result in some interesting volunteer problems. First, you will probably have a mixture of volunteer leaders from all participating merger partners. These new leaders will need to determine how to work together and adjust to new leadership styles. Second, new volunteers from outside the organizational culture may be joining the group that could impact "business as usual" meetings. Third, melding two or more entities with different operational, decision-making, and policy styles will require the patience and understanding of all.

Last, there will usually be a core group of former volunteers who perceive that there is no longer a place for them in the new organization. Giving special attention to this group, so as not to lose volunteer base at the highest level of the organization, will pay benefits in the long run. Techniques used to keep this cadre of volunteers involved include:

- Continue to send former board members information on a regular basis
- Mail summaries of past and pending board policy activities
- Mail an annual report
- Develop a VIP newsletter

- Invite the group to various functions

- Recruit them to serve on high-level committees

- Provide recognition opportunities (emeritus or honorary status, etc.)

POSTMERGER OPERATIONS

Determining what operational components to merge is a process that is unique to each merger. However, some guidelines may help select a place to start.

Personnel/Payroll

It is usually advisable to begin early to get personnel and payroll under one management. This effort not only will result in some small cost savings but will ensure a more consistent application of personnel policies.

During this transitional process, you may need some additional assistance. For example, if the salary and benefits options for the premerged entities were widely disparate, a wage and benefits survey by an independent agency may be of help. A usual technique is to bring all employees up to the more rewarding plan. However, this may not be economically feasible. Looking for solutions like a gradual move toward wage and benefit parity may be a better answer. Considering the example of several airline company mergers and their labor difficulties, it is best not to schedule a wage and benefits equality model that takes too long to fulfill.

Accounting

It is important to combine accounting (especially funds handling) as soon as practical in order to gain some economies of scale, as well as to reduce audit costs. Further, part of increasing capacity is to meld budget line items. In addition, you will want clean accounting periods to have data that will help to evaluate the progress of the merger.

Accounting melding is usually more of a back room exercise than one that will require a significant amount of executive time. If the new organization is one in which funds will be collected and deposited in a variety of places, some sophisticated mechanics for sweeping funds into corporate accounts may be required. Controls of cash will require attention. Also, signature authority for the ability of the new organization to contract and manage spending levels should be examined. Some organizations may allow certain staff levels the authority to spend up to a specific amount of money without approval from a higher level of management. These policies should be reviewed to avoid a surprise at a later date. Also, look at the spending limits the CEO is granted by the board of directors. It is usually necessary to raise the single-signature limit in a merged organization that may be many times larger that any of the individual organizations pre-merger.

CHAPTER 9

Evaluation and Stewardship

EVALUATION

E VALUATING THE RESULTS of a merger in the short term is difficult at best, and in some cases almost impossible. Yet, board members and volunteers are eager to find confirmation that their decisions were justified and correct. Frequently, senior staff feel the need to check the merger process and show empirical evidence of the soundness of the idea and value of the effort. McLaughlin (1996) explains: "The real integration occurs after the merger is formalized, and this period must be measured in years. Indeed, it can be argued that the post-merger period extends indefinitely, as both parties learn about each other in the process of creating a new, shared identity" (p. 25). He also recommends that you solicit an independent evaluation 12–24 months into the merger and evaluate the success of mutually agreed-upon goals (p. 23). A study by Singer and Yankey (1991) that examined 18 mergers, acquisitions, and consolidations among nonprofit organizations showed that no formal evaluations were done because board members and executives did not regard evaluation as a high priority (p. 368). However, evaluation is crucial for the future health of your new organization.

There are basically only three areas that will give you any indications of efficacy post-merger. These are: financial, operational practice, and mission impact. In any evaluation effort, it is important to note that unless there is some form of data that can be compared objectively, the evaluation will be anecdotal or observational based, and therefore not an accurate indicator of the result of the merger.

Unfortunately, the nature of the mission for many nonprofit organizations (NPOs) makes any type of impact measurement difficult. Frequently, the result of an NPO's work is not known for many years or is such that determining a direct act vs. result comparison is impossible. An example might be: an environmental organization that purchases land to protect a specific species of plant or animal. The NPO may not know if the act made any difference for decades, or if it had a major impact on the problem. Organizations with very specific goals and objectives that can be measured mechanically by their own data or data compiled by others have a better opportunity to ascertain the result of a merger than those that do not.

Measuring financial results of a merger is also more difficult than first appears. It seems simple to add figures for gross revenue and direct costs to see if an organization is better off. However, many of the costs of the merger will appear in the first 6 to 18 months, and thus interfere with an accurate postmerger financial picture. This factor is compounded by the tendency of NPOs to account for employee time using some system of functional allocation. Function allocation is a process by which employees that have significant autonomy over their time allocate portions of their time to individual tasks or programs. In such a system, the staff time used in a merger or how staff is deployed postmerger may not accurately reflect how they really work.

The advantages of other financial changes may also take a long time to appear on an organization's bottom line. These include the cost of restructuring leases, closing facilities, acquiring new facilities, and negotiating new mortgages and loan agreements. Another major impediment to accurate financial measurement of the impact of merger is the human resource redeployment. Most mergers create a significant shift in how people work, who does what, and even how many will work post-merger. This process takes many months and in some cases a year or more to sort out. It is not uncommon for NPOs to carry employee-heavy tables of organization through a merger transition period with the expectation that the issue will take care of itself in the months to come.

Because many types of contracts such as payroll handling or phone services cannot effectively be negotiated until after the merger is complete, the potential savings from these ventures will also lag during the event and delay an accurate evaluation of the merger.

The impact on business practice is also difficult to evaluate. Earlier in this book, the question of "What happens on the first day after the merger?" was answered with the response: "Very little." Any gain from improved or more efficient business practices will also be delayed, thus putting off evaluation even further downstream.

There are some points to evaluate early that at least give some indication as to what the merger provides. While these measures may not tell whether the organization is doing what it is supposed to be doing or whether it is doing better, it can show what it is doing differently. These differences could be perceived as surrogate measures for what is anticipated to be important or an advantage as the merged organization progresses. These include:

Overall Financial Capacity

This notion might be akin to what individuals refer to as net worth or companies refer to as net asset value (NAV). Highly simplified, NAV equals the total value of all assets minus debt and known financial obligations. A quick look at this number will give an organization a snapshot of post-merger equity vs. debt. While not a measure of merger potential, it is at least a baseline from which future financial posture can be compared.

Most audit reports from the premerged entities can show this number in aggregate from previous years.

Volunteers and Members

Surprisingly, many organizations do not have an accurate count of how many volunteers they have working on their behalf. Also, attempting to place value on volunteer services is practically impossible. Some entities have attempted to qualify volunteers using a term called "lifetime value" that tries to combine a volunteer's cash donation total with services over time. Placing a conjectural value on what it would cost an organization if it were to pay for the services provided by one or more volunteers is not a productive exercise. Further, the resultant value, being artificial, is highly subjective. However, if organizations know how many volunteers they have, combining the volunteer count from all merged partners will provide an idea about work capacity when compared to premerger numbers. This number could be revisited to see if the new organization is increasing or decreasing volunteer counts.

Membership is usually easier to determine. Members, especially if membership is for fee or dues, can be measured with a value of both numbers and dollars. The immediate financial value of members is one measurement. Membership trend is another. Thinking of membership in terms of capacity and potential provides a merged entity with extremely important planning data. For example, if the combined organizations offer members new incentives and advantages to belong, there can be a case made for increasing dues. Thus, even after contemplating some loss in membership because of raising prices (a common occurrence), there is a potential for more gross revenue. As an aside, organizations lose members when they raise prices not necessarily because it costs more, but because it causes members to reconsider their participation decision. Thus, members who have been renewing automatically for years may drop out.

From the evaluation perspective, membership counts, like many other measurements, are important because they provide a merger database number for future trending. While it would not be considered unusual for merged entities to experience a loss in membership early on, if the trend continues, it is an indication for needed change.

Increased Efficiencies

Merged entities can sometimes evaluate the act using increased efficiency measures. These fall into two categories: direct efficiencies and efficiencies due to the economies of scale.

Direct efficiencies are those derived simply from closing capacity. An example would be: two organizations each have a home office. Post-merger, one office will be closed and its capacity absorbed into the remaining facility. In this case, the direct efficiency is the amount of lease or rent plus any other operation and maintenance costs associated with the closing facility. In a recent merger, an NPO with one midsize facility merged with an NPO that had eight offices in a four-state region. The larger entity was able to redistribute the one midsize operation among its existing offices, resulting in immediate net savings of more than $250,000.

Economies of scale efficiencies refers simply to buying and negotiations power based on size. To maximize the result of a merger, an organization should begin this process immediately. Actually negotiating economies of scale "deals" pre-merger is a good idea. The concept is simple: unit cost of certain goods and services is less when unit count increases. Renegotiating service contracts, printing costs, insurance policies, marketing costs, image-building items like tee shirts and other logo-related things is a good starting point.

When this process begins premerger, the resultant savings can be described as an evaluation component to demonstrate the wisdom of doing the merger. Projecting these types of efficiencies into the future shows the real power of merger.

Redeployment of Critical Staff

As mentioned previously in this book, the redeployment of staff into critical mission-related or mission-enabling areas is one of the primary drivers for organizations to merge in the first place. Likewise, the potential shift in staff application is also a significant evaluation point. Make sure to get an accurate count of how staff is deployed premerger. Then, post-merger, after an organization has moved people into mission-critical or mission-enabling positions, recount and compare the numbers. For the most part, the resultant merged organization should have more people in mission-critical positions, like service delivery, and mission-enabling positions, like fundraising activities, and fewer in administration. This type of evaluation is very popular with volunteers, boards of directors, and donors.

Avoid measures and evaluations that are merely interesting to know or that do not speak to an organization's potential or enhanced capacity. Evaluation is a time-consuming process and can be expensive to implement. Select a few critical components that focus on before-and-after merger rather than on what is happening now and what is expected to happen later. Measures should show how an organization manages and responds to the merger, not necessarily evaluate the soundness of the merger decision.

Another merger evaluation issue is data interpretation, trying to determine what numbers would be considered good or bad. Is an initial net loss necessarily bad? Does an organization need an initial net gain of x percent to justify the act of merger? As might be expected, these questions can only be answered in context. For example, if viability or organizational survivability is in question, the value of merger would be measured on a very different scale than if viable organizations are merging to achieve a competitive advantage. This idea suggests that evaluation and subsequently the points upon which evaluation is based are unique to each organization. Looking at several measures, it appears that an organization can save about 4% of its gross budget in the first year. This number could be higher if saving money is one of the primary objectives of the merger.

A last thought on evaluation is to look for measures that can be ongoing rather than one-glance measures that may not be meaningful in the long term. Measurement should provide an indication of the health and well-being of an organization rather than attempt to justify or discredit the act of merger. Measure what the result of the merger is. Do not evaluate the decision to merge. Postmerger it is too late to reconsider the decision.

STEWARDSHIP

The concept of stewardship is unique to nonprofit and religious organizations. It refers to an organization operating in a manner that would stand up to a test or great scrutiny by its donors and constituents. Stewardship includes financial as well as mission integrity. In mergers, both financial and mission issues relate to stewardship. For-profit organizations think of stewardship as share value. Stewardship is more emotional with a monetary twist.

From a strictly financial perspective, it is critical that the newly merged organization expects to be better off postmerger, or at least within the near term, than premerger. Informing members and constituents of the financial impact of the merger is an important and critical stewardship exercise. An organization should not fear its volunteers and donors questioning the aspects of a merger, and that is why early information and educational efforts are required. If the organization expects the merger to result in a financial loss for some period, let your constituents know and explain why this fact is in the best interest of the entity long term. Likewise, if there is an anticipated financial boost or some stabilization of revenue and expenses as a result of merger, that is also a stewardship issue that can work to the advantage of the organization if properly used.

Stewardship also includes showing the friends and supporters of an organization that its leadership is doing all it can to make the organization better. Do not be concerned that constituents will ask "if merger is such a great idea, why didn't you do it before now?" This type of thinking is no more productive than asking why the computer wasn't invented in 1900. The opportunity, circumstances, and leadership were in place at this time and the organization elected to move. Keep the perspective that the concept is new and obviously viable, and now is the time for our organization to merge. Additionally, do not hesitate to proclaim the success and efficiencies a merger brings to an organization. This alone is an act of stewardship. Making an organization better, more efficient, more mission effective, and able to continue to prosper are all acts of stewardship. The list below shows areas of stewardship and evaluation points.

- Employees continue to be informed through various means (e-mail, newsletters, staff meetings) of merger progress

- Letterhead/logo is revised (if required)

- Local, state, and national media are informed

- News release and news events are presented as evidence of public awareness

- Redeployment of people is announced (who moved where to do what and why)

- Pre/postmerger staff allocation

- Pre/postmerger staff numbers and cost (related to program/services)

- Reallocation of resources (money moved, not saved)

- Shifts in budget emphasis

- Programmatic changes

- New initiatives made possible by merger

- Reduction of duplication

- Activities that have been decommissioned

- Reacquaintance of donors and constituencies

- Pre/postmerger member/constituency numbers (separate and combined)

- Pre/postmerger donor base

- Pre/postmerger total fundraising

- Pre/postmerger volunteer involvement

Stewardship and evaluation are not only desirable, but absolutely critical in the postmerger environment. Plan and budget for evaluation and stewardship costs and programs. Without a formalized effort in this area, your organization may never know if the merger was ultimately in its best interest, but more importantly, may not make the indicated modifications to capitalize on the opportunities merger presents.

REFERENCES

McLaughlin, T. A. (1996). *Seven steps to a successful nonprofit merger*. Washington, DC: National Center for Nonprofit Boards.

Singer, M.J. & Yankey, J.A. (1991). Organizational metamorphosis: A study of eighteen nonprofit mergers, acquisitions, and consolidations. *Nonprofit Management & Leadership*, *1*(4), 357-369.

Conclusion

I N CONCLUSION, the merger of nonprofit organizations is a complex exercise in emotional, technical, and organizational change. Every organization is unique and will experience a unique set and subset of merger issues, problems, opportunities, and joys. The melding of nonprofits into common interest organizations is a coming trend that will totally redefine the nonprofit organizational landscape. Those that are agile will survive and prosper. Those that are not will lose mission components as they are swept away in this massive reorganization wave rather than learn to ride with the rising tide.

The following chart summarizes the process. The technique for accomplishing the 10 points presented below is not simple or easy. The task is to plan early, be proactive, and make sure you have skilled assistance to guide you and your organization up the mountain of success and avoid the abyss of failure. Figure 1 shows a flowchart for mergers.

This book has shown what you can expect to encounter when you move your organization toward merger, including how to find a potential merger partner, the technical and emotional nature of mergers, the costs and timing of mergers, and possible

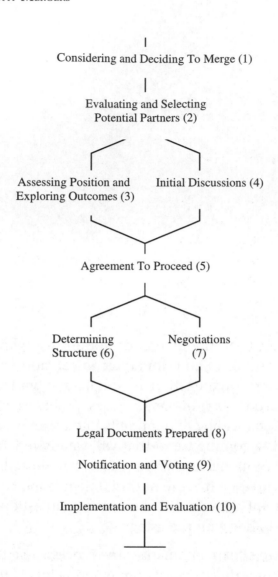

Figure 1 Nonprofit Merger Flowchart

techniques and approaches that can make for a positive merger experience. Examples show how others have survived, and even flourished, pre- and post-merger. Although the benefits that may be achieved through merger are unknown, experience shows that you can plan, project, and create pro forma until the opportunity to merge is long gone and still not know for sure what the ultimate outcome will be. Among the expected benefits are immediately increased capacity and a chance to do more to support the organization's mission. It is hoped that the decision to merge will serve the organization well beyond this time. That is the promise of merger: more, more efficiently, more capable, more longevity, and a better organization at the end of not just the day, but every day.

Mergers are usually not easy. In some cases, merger is truly the only option for survival, yet organizations continue to resist. Mergers nearly always leave some staff and volunteers in their wake. Losses of essential senior level staff and some longtime productive volunteers are almost a given. Sometimes leadership must guide an organization in a direction that may not be popular. In the case study of the American Cancer Society in Appendix B, many volunteers and staff were resistant, and were even direct impediments to merger, yet the organization, led by a courageous team of senior-level management, continued the course. The results: an organization that is more financially sound, reaching new highs in fund-raising annually, increasing volunteer involvement, and more agile in re-action to market forces than ever before. That is the prize.

There is an old saying that "ships are safe in port, but that is not why they are built." Merger is a time for leadership to set sail and captain the organization to a new land. A land of opportunity is made available by the increased capacity of merger with a dynamic partner.

Windstar Foundation— A Case History

THE WINDSTAR FOUNDATION was the philanthropic brainchild of singer-songwriter John Denver. Denver was noted for his commitment to world peace, world hunger, and environmental causes. In 1984 he and a small group of friends established the Windstar Foundation to be a "catalyst for responsible environmental action by all people."

The Foundation was seeded with nearly $3 million of Denver's personal funds. Almost immediately, the Foundation purchased 1,500 acres of pristine mountain and valley land near Aspen, CO. It built a modest headquarters building and hired a small staff. The Foundation started on its quest to attract members and friends of similar interest. It also developed a biodome. The biodome was a geodesic dome inspired by the models of Buckminster Fuller and designed to be a solar greenhouse for growing food. The intent of the dome was to provide families a way to grow their own vegetables year-round, thus meeting their needs themselves. In the early days, both of these ventures proved to be successful.

In 1986, the Foundation held its first symposium. It attracted supporters and friends to Aspen each August for this event that was designed to elevate awareness and stimulate others to "act locally and think globally" about the environment and other critical world issues.

From the beginning, the events became a financial drain. In an effort to produce a major activity that would attract paying participants, the cost became overwhelming and the Foundation began to lose serious money.

In 1987, the Foundation reorganized and increased the size of its board of directors from 3 to 15. This new energy produced additional funds and increased support in general, but not enough, quickly enough.

The board and staff believed the symposium would eventually prove profitable. They continued to hold the event and lost money steadily for five years. The board of directors authorized borrowing money to sustain operations from a bank using the Windstar land as collateral. This proved to be the point of no return for the Foundation. Within three years, the Foundation was faced with declining membership, reduced attendance at the symposium, and a debt load in excess of $500,000. Indeed, the Foundation was not sustaining itself.

Adding to the difficulties was a rapid turnover in top staff positions as well as a small donor base that was becoming fatigued. The annual financial shortfall was approaching $200,000.

The Foundation had ignored the warning signs of the survivability spiral and now was faced with dissolution. The only options at this time were to dissolve or try to find a merger partner.

Dissolution was actually not an option. If the Foundation were to dissolve, that event would be widely publicized because of its connection to John Denver; there was the potential for damage to his image and career. The organization had to find another solution. With pressure mounting from creditors and no consistent leadership, the Foundation began in earnest to seek a partner.

At this time, the National Wildlife Federation (NWF) entered the scene. In 1990, NWF was an organization with an annual budget of almost $90 million and growing. A worldwide membership and substantial political presence in Washington, DC, made NWF a formidable force in the wildlife and environmental arena. NWF had what Windstar needed—the ability to infuse significant cash into its mission and relieve the burden of debt service.

Windstar had two primary desirable assets. One was the land in Aspen. The land was valuable as a preserve, but long-term restrictions placed on the land by Pitkin County (CO) authorities limiting its development potential reduced its value to the Windstar Foundation as a marketable asset. Further, the philosophy of the Foundation was to protect the land to fulfill its mission of ecology, not use it for financial advancement.

The second asset of the Windstar Foundation was the commitment and interest of John Denver. Denver was an active participant in the Windstar Foundation, served on its board of directors, made significant financial contributions to the Foundation, and was interested and engaged in the Foundation's work. Denver's name was attached to the Foundation and he was an ambassador for it at every turn.

However, he was unwilling simply to bail out the Foundation with a large influx of money. His philosophy was that if the Foundation could not sustain its activities through its operation, then it may have outlived its viability.

The negotiation with NWF began simply enough, with representatives from both organizations present. From the outset, it was evident that the merger would result in a significant loss of autonomy for the Foundation. As the negotiations continued, Windstar's debt load continued to mount, putting additional pressure on its board for a quick settlement.

In the end, NWF agreed to assume the debt for title to the land. It further agreed to keep the land as a preserve. It assumed all assets, patents, and rights owned by the Foundation. The most difficult component to accept was the replacement of the Windstar board of directors with a seven-person board that included Denver, two representatives from the former Windstar board, and four members appointed by the chief executive officer of the NWF. In addition, Denver agreed to become a spokesperson for NWF.

The Windstar Foundation case is a perfect example of an organization that found itself in a position of having to accept what was offered or lose its identity and the opportunity to further its cause. With hindsight, it's clear that cutting back operations until more favorable funding existed, avoiding leveraging its assets, and recognizing early signs of financial trouble such as membership decline could have prevented the need to merge or at least put Windstar in a better negotiating posture.

This example points out how easy it is for a well-meaning, capable board of directors to make decisions that could be characterized as more emotionally based than steeped in facts. In retrospect, the odds of the Foundation raising the level of funds needed, when historically it had never done so, was a long shot at best.

The mission was good and the cause just. There were many hard-working, well-meaning, committed board members and volunteers. Yet all of that was not enough. In Windstar's case, the economics did not support the vision.

American Cancer Society—A Case History

I N 1995, the American Cancer Society (ACS) began a reorganizational journey that resulted in reshaping every aspect of the organization and setting the stage for a new paradigm in nonprofit structure. The ACS called it resource realignment, to reflect the intent to reapportion the way in which dollars were spent, resulting in the realignment of resources away from organizational and structural initiatives and toward increased mission delivery. The following is an account of the strategic development and implementation process that resulted in merging 57 separate corporate entities (divisions) into 17 regional organizations.

HISTORICAL PERSPECTIVE

The premerger divisional structure of the American Cancer Society was originally established in the 1940s. Since that time, the ACS has grown into the largest voluntary health organization in the world in terms of number of volunteers (2 million) and the amount of money the organization raises annually ($670 million). Over time, the organization has had to face major changes from both within and without. Within the ACS, the nature of its volunteer-based philosophy of large volunteer involvement grew to the point at which restructuring was not only desired but also imperative to the survival of the organization. In 1992, when restructuring discussions began, the national board of directors of the ACS had more than 250 members. These board members represented various American Cancer Society state divisions, with representation proportionally based on population. This national governance model had grown to be extraordinarily cumbersome, fraught with the political realities of any large organization, and difficult and expensive to maintain. Within the individual state divisions, the same problems existed on a smaller scale. For example, the Nebraska division, with a population of 1,578,385 (1990 census), had 55 members on the board of directors. Maine had 47 members in its House of Delegates and 36 members on its board of directors, charged with operating a $3 million corporation. Rhode Island had a board of directors of 36 with a budget of $1 million. In all these cases, the scale of directorship greatly outstretched the size of the entity being managed.

Additionally, each division had a chief executive officer, a complement of senior program and fundraising staff, and a full administrative staff, plus a large number of volunteers providing administrative support, conducting programs, and directing fundraising events. In each of these state operations there were duplications in a variety of activities such as financial oversight, information systems, warehousing and distributions of materials, and mission-related programs and services. Similar structural components existed in each of the Society's 57 divisions even though they represented a disparate revenue capacity—from $200,000 to $43 million—and were diverse geographically, encompassing all the states, several large cities, and Puerto Rico. By 1991, it became clear that the infrastructure to support volunteers and programs had grown too difficult and expensive to maintain in its current state.

Another issue was the widening difference in the ability of individual divisions to respond to the macro mission of the ACS. This disparity among divisional capacity became the living force for change. The idea took hold that, if there were large, high-capacity regional entities, the organization could give the primary segments of its constituencies a more consistent and complete array of services.

MOTIVATION AND PRIMARY DRIVING FORCE FOR CHANGE

These realizations started a double-pronged approach of change in the Society. First, using volunteer committees staffed by the field operations department, the organization identified the strategic reasons for realignment and restructuring. Second, a plan was made to achieve these changes on two levels. On the first level, the plan involved the reorganization of the national governance structure (including reduction of the size of the board of directors) and the corporate office, including reengineering its program, fundraising, and administrative structures. On the second level, the ACS began the resource realignment process in its individual state and local divisions.

STRATEGIC REASONS TO MERGE

The original strategic plan directed five primary initiatives. The first directive was: "Establish leadership in the delivery of cancer information." This mandated the creation of local call centers that would be networked with a national call center. The local call centers would allow for the entire country to have instant access to all ACS programs, services, and information, delivered in one consistent voice.

The second directive was to provide local leadership in cancer prevention and control nationwide through enhanced collaboration with others, transforming state-of-the-science and state-of-the-art into state-of-the-practice. This was an attempt to address the aforementioned problem where the application of ACS services was inconsistent from state to state. The creation of interdivisional program staff specialists with appropriate knowledge, training, and support would allow for sophisticated programs that met targeted audiences' needs. A greater yield on investment can occur when attention is given to high-priority cancer groups within large populations. The Society's ability to create external collaborations with the cancer control community gives it leverage.

The third directive was: "Develop, support and market a focused high-impact cancer research program which complements, but does not duplicate others." Over the past decade, ACS income was relatively flat, hampering its ability to foster and support increasingly expensive and expanding research programs. This directive to support research could only be met with additional income. Resource realignment, which allows more staff to move to a community level where volunteers assigned to fundraising can be given more support, seemed to be an appropriate method to satisfy this directive.

The fourth directive stated: "Advocate aggressively at both local and national levels on behalf of cancer patients and cancer control." This recognizes that advocacy can best be supported through the development of volunteer-based networks at the local level. This effort requires more local staff support and the purchase of communications technologies that many divisions do not have. The ACS realized that regional coordination of focused, strategically aligned advocacy efforts would greatly enhance fulfillment of its mission.

The fifth directive was: "Adopt best practices, with built-in accountability, for the acquisition and development of resources, both human and financial." Adopting this directive recognized leadership's belief that the ACS needed to shift from a product-driven to a market- and donor-driven orientation. Marketing itself as a cause-related organization meant that the ACS needed to develop staff expertise in fundraising areas such as solicitation of major gifts and initiatives via the Internet, to attract the resources to meet its objectives.

As a prelude to launching resource realignment, a committee began to rework the national mission statement, which resulted in the following: *The American Cancer Society is the nationwide community-based voluntary health organization dedicated to eliminating cancer as a major health problem by preventing cancer, saving lives and diminishing suffering from cancer, through research, education, advocacy, and service.* By revising its mission and reshaping its organizational structure to accomplish this mission, an essential philosophical shift occurred. The realignment of the Society allowed for priority attention to cancer control by reducing the focus on governance and organizational efforts. The resulting changes in structure created a tightly focused, outcome based, strategic board designed to redirect the organization to new levels of productivity.

STRATEGIC GOAL

The five strategic directives discussed above gave birth to the essential goal that has become the underpinning of the mission as well as the basis for the resource realignment initiative. That goal is simple: To reduce deaths from cancer by 50% and incidence by 25% by the year 2015.

It was apparent that the lack of growth in revenue and volunteerism currently being experienced by the Society would not allow it to achieve this essential goal. Since 1984, the gross fundraising of the ACS had not kept pace with increases in the consumer price index. Planning for growth, the ACS was not able to curtail loss in almost every measurement within the organization. However, its overall financial health was, and continues to be, solid because of its fundraising philosophy. Each year expenditures match funds raised from the preceding year, and the annual budget is restricted to no more than 110% of the previous year's revenue. Although this conservative approach to budgeting kept the ACS financially in the black, income statistics demonstrated it was not showing healthy growth from year to year. While operating in a fiscally responsible manner, the organization none the less had to absorb the increasing costs of doing business, sometimes at the expense of mission delivery. This was recognized as unacceptable and has fostered change that is already marked by substantial revenue increases and expansion of mission-related activity.

A national shift in demographics of volunteers and donors also played a part in the lack of growth for the ACS. The profile of those who donate to philanthropic organizations demonstrates that the average age of donors is increasing. The ACS discovered it needed to cultivate a relationship with a younger segment of the population to encourage their monetary gifts and secure new volunteers. This aging donor and volunteer base would eventually need to replace itself.

In evaluating the move to resource realignment, the American Cancer Society also had to consider the increase in donor competition it was facing from organizations with similar objectives to its own. When the ACS compared itself to other health care not-for-profits, it found its market share of the total philanthropic dollar was decreasing, as well as its share in the percentage of volunteers. The number of nonprofit organizations raising money to fight cancer has grown sharply in recent years. As of this writing, 47 national organizations have the word "cancer" in their names. The proliferation of newer volunteer organizations that addressed other life-threatening illnesses, such as AIDS, contributed to declining volunteerism within the ACS. To emerge as the leading organization in cancer education and research and meet the stated goal, the ACS needed to recognize its major competitors and adjust its fundraising and volunteer recruitment efforts appropriately. The resource realignment initiative was the answer.

CULTURAL BARRIER

Because the American Cancer Society was a volunteer-based organization with 57 separate corporate divisions, the executives of each division enjoyed a great deal of autonomy. "You can change anything in a nonprofit organization except tradition" (Clint Clampitt, national vice president, eastern field operations, the American Cancer Society). A varying number of additional representatives from each division—staff and volunteers—were also involved in decision-making. It was proving increasingly difficult to have effective divisional leadership that could bring focused and meaningful input to the larger decision-making processes of the ACS. By changing to only 17 geographic components, the ACS could subset representatives into essential areas of interest. It could also bring in leaders who work every day in the field to ensure that input from all levels and each division is influencing the larger organization's strategic direction. This concept resulted in a not-too-subtle shift from a volunteer-driven organization to one that recognizes critical volunteer and staff partnership that must exist in today's not-for-profit environment. This partnership clearly delineates the strategic, outcome-focused role of volunteer board members in establishing organization policies and activities of volunteers and staff.

PROCESS

Over the course of two years, staff and volunteers from the field operations department of the American Cancer Society national office headed up a group of volunteer board members, staff members, and others. Their job was to evaluate the need for resource realignment. After studying the available data, this group concluded that the ACS had become too organizationally focused, was top heavy in its administrative structure both nationally and in the field, and needed to place more staff and support resources into the true field. The true field is the location where organizational structure makes direct contact with volunteers and users of services and where major components of mission program delivery and income generation take place.

When the chief executive officer received this report, he initiated a process to design the new organizational model. Any field division office that had less than approximately $10 million in gross revenue from all income sources was probably too small to survive on its own. If its revenue growth remained constant, it certainly would not have sufficient resource capacity to meet the demands in cancer control that the Society set for itself into the new millenium. Clearly, the ACS needed to consolidate its offices into entities that were larger than $10 million (later benchmarked at $15–20 million).

The next step was to create an environment in which these organizations could begin to talk with each other about how they could join together. Remember, divisions had been independently incorporated with semiautonomous governance structures to use its name and shelter under its nonprofit tax status. The national office was reluctant to dictate reorganization structure or process. Facilitating the process of resource realignment without disrupting the volunteer and staff spirit and reducing fund development was another vital consideration in choosing the technique of merger implementation.

The task was to consider how to persuade the broad number of volunteers, many of whom held prestigious positions, including voting rights, to relinquish local control of traditional operations that over the years had been built with much state geographic pride. The question was one of transferring American Cancer Society loyalty, often identified with, and solidified by, state boundaries, to a new concept of regionalization. The challenge was to win their support and their votes for a plan that would result in consolidation. This highly political process became the major component of the nontechnical aspects of the merger and, frankly, the key to volunteer and staff acceptance of the proposed merger.

The first step of the resource realignment merger was to obtain the willing cooperation of boards of directors and the membership within various divisions. This was done by explaining the rationale behind resources realignment, educating key people on central questions, and encouraging the political process that would ensure a favorable vote. This human-centered part of the merger was central to the process. Since each division was an independent corporate entity, an affirmative directorship or membership vote was required, or legally the mergers could not occur.

The ACS began the process by launching on three fronts. First, divisions without sufficient capacity for the future were identified and attached to a stronger division. In order to reduce resistance yet initiate the change process, a tiered plan allowed divisions to create a continuing change, which over time would meet the resource realignment objectives. The result of its first effort was to create a multiyear contract under which a committee comprised of representatives from seven separate state divisions would jointly operate a region. The second effort was to continue to provide venues where volunteers and staff (facilitated by field operations department staff) could conduct research, data collection, and analysis to study the potential gains to be had through resource realignment, and to build a case study for the initiative for local boards and volunteers.

Next, divisions that entered into merger talks early were helped by field operation staff leadership teams to explore what could be achieved by the realignment and merging of resources and the reduction of redundancies. Soon several divisions were moving toward mergers using these processes.

The amazing results are that, as of this writing, almost three years after the initial joint operation, all but two of the divisions that met the original profile are either merged or are in merger negotiations.

The commitment to process and respect for the culture of the organization allowed the ACS field operations department, under the leadership of John Seffrin, PhD, chief executive officers and Donald Thomas, chief operating officer, and national vice presidents Bill Barram and Clint Clampitt, to present senior volunteer staff the compelling message that made merger a reality and resculpted the landscape of the American Cancer Society forever.

Table B–1 Division Merger Vote Requirement

	ACS Iowa	ACS Minnesota	ACS Wisconsin	ACS South Dakota
Notice to Board	10 days	5 days	20 days	10 days prior to meeting
Board Quorum	1/3 of the members	1/3 total number of board of directors	1/3 total membership	Majority of the members
Board Vote	Majority of all directors	Majority of all directors members	Majority of votes cast at a meeting at which a quorum is present	Majority of directors in office
Notice to Members	N/A	Not less than 10 nor more than 30 days	21 days	N/A
Member Quorum	N/A	35 voting members representing at least 5 units	1/3 total membership	N/A
Member Vote	N/A	Majority of votes cast at a meeting at which a quorum is present	2/3 votes cast at a meeting at which a quorum is present	N/A

Sample Notice of Meetings

MEMORANDUM

Date:

To:

From:

Re: Meeting notice information

Here are the merger documents required for consideration at your Board of Directors meetings. Please send the items listed below to your members in accordance with your regular meeting notice, ensuring the minimum notice on the attached chart is observed.

1. Plan of Merger

2. Resolutions for Directors

3. Copy of the Bylaws

Sample Plan and Agreement To Merge

PLAN OF MERGER
BETWEEN
(NAME OF CORPORATION)
AND
(NAME OF CORPORATION)

THIS PLAN OF MERGER is made this ___day of _____, 2000, by and between _____, a (State) nonprofit corporation and _____, a (State) nonprofit corporation.

1.   Recitals. The respective boards of directors of _____ and _____ deem it advisable that the corporations merge into a single corporation as hereinafter specified. Each of _____ and _____ is recognized as exempt under Section 501(c)(3) of the Internal Revenue Code of 1986, as amended, and is a nonstock corporation.

2.   Constituent Corporations. The name and state of incorporation of each constituent corporation are as follows:

Name

State
of Incorporation

3.   Terms and Conditions. The terms and conditions of the merger are as follows:

(a) On the ___ day of _____, 2000, at 12:01 a.m.,
which shall be the Effective Date, _____ shall be merged into
_____, which shall be the surviving corporation.

(b) The Articles of Incorporation of _____
shall be and remain the articles of incorporation of the surviving corporation until the same shall be altered, amended or repealed or provided therein or as otherwise provided by law.

(c) The bylaws of _____ that are effective
as of the Effective Date (the "Bylaws") shall be and remain the Bylaws
of the surviving corporation until the same shall be altered, amended
or repealed as therein provided or as otherwise provided by law.

(d) As of the Effective Date, the number of directors which shall constitute the entire board of _____ shall be
_____ (__), and the Bylaws of _____ shall be amended
to reflect the increase in directors and to indicate _____ (__) directors
shall be representatives of _____ as of the Effective Date of the
merger.

(e) This merger shall become effective upon the
Effective Date.

(f) On or after the Effective Date:

i) _____ is intended to and shall
succeed to the rights of _____ and _____ to any gifts or
bequests.

ii) _____ shall continue the
charitable work previously performed in the States of _____, by
_____ and _____, respectively; and

iii) All funds held by _____ which are attributable to _____ and _____ will continue to be used in conformity with the express intent of the donors of such funds, if any such intent has been specified.

(g) No member of the board of directors _____ or _____ shall receive or keep anything as a result of the merger.

4.   <u>Mode of Carrying Into Effect</u>. The mode of carrying the terms and conditions of the merger into effect shall be as follows:

(a) On the Effective Date, _____ shall be merged into _____, the separate existence of _____ shall cease, and _____ shall continue in existence; such merger shall in all respects have the effect provided for a statutory merger under laws of _____ and _____.

(b) _____ and _____ shall take all necessary or appropriate action in order to effectuate the merger. At any time after the Effective Date, in the event that _____ shall consider any assignments, conveyances, assurances or other acts to be necessary or desirable in order to carry out the provisions hereof, the proper officers, directors and trustees of _____ and _____ shall execute and deliver any and all documents and do all things necessary or proper to carry out the provisions hereof.

5. <u>Manner of Converting Memberships</u>. There are no members of _____, and on and after the Effective Date, _____ will continue to remain without members. Consequently, the membership's interests of the members of _____ shall automatically expire, without any separate consideration or exchange therefor.

6. <u>Approval</u>. This Plan of Merger shall be approved by _____ and _____ in the manner provided by the applicable laws of the States of _____ and _____, re-

spectively, and in accordance with their respective articles of incorporation and bylaws.

7. <u>State Filings</u>. After approval by _____ and _____ in accordance with the manner set forth above, Articles of Merger shall be filed as required by the laws of the States of _____ and _____.

8. <u>Amendment or Abandonment</u>. At any time prior to filing the Articles of Merger, the respective boards of directors of _____ and _____ are authorized to amend this Plan of Merger as permitted by law or to abandon this Plan of Merger.

9. <u>Qualification to Transact Business</u>. _____ shall obtain any necessary authority to transact business as a foreign nonprofit corporation in _____.

Sample Resolutions

PROPOSED RESOLUTIONS FOR BOARD OF DIRECTORS
OF
(NAME)

WHEREAS, the Board of Directors has reviewed the Plan of Merger attached hereto as Exhibit "A" (the "Plan of Merger"), among (Names of Corporations);

RESOLVED, the Board of Directors hereby adopts and approves the Plan of Merger substantially in the form attached;

RESOLVED, that the Plan of Merger be submitted to the members of (Name of Corporation) as provided by the (State) Nonprofit Corporation Act;

RESOLVED, that upon the approval of the Plan of Merger by a majority of votes cast by the members of (Name of Corporation) present at a meeting at which quorum is present, the Chairman of the Board, the President or any Vice President and the Secretary or any Assistant Secretary are, and each of them is hereby authorized, empowered and directed to execute on behalf of (Name of Corporation) Certificates of

Merger and such other documents and take such further actions which may be reasonably necessary to consummate the transactions contemplated by the Plan of Merger, including, without limitation, effecting such amendments and modifications to the Plan of Merger as may be necessary to consummate the transactions contemplated thereby.

**PROPOSED RESOLUTIONS FOR MEMBERS
OF
(NAME)**

WHEREAS, the Board of Directors has adopted the Plan of Merger attached hereto as Exhibit "A" (the "Plan of Merger") among (Names of Corporations);

RESOLVED, the members of (Name of Corporation) hereby adopt and approve the Plan of Merger substantially in the form attached;

RESOLVED, the officers of the Board of Directors of (Name of Corporation) are, and each of them is hereby authorized, empowered and directed to execute on behalf of (Name of Corporation) Certificates of Merger and such other documents and take such further actions which may be reasonably necessary to consummate the transactions contemplated by the Plan of Merger, including, without limitation, effecting such amendments and modifications to the Plan of Merger as may be necessary to consummate the transactions contemplated thereby.

Sample Articles of Merger

ARTICLES OF MERGER
MERGING
(NAME OF ORGANIZATION)
INTO
(NAME OF ORGANIZATION)

The undersigned corporation, for the purpose of merging (Name of Organization), a (State) nonprofit corporation, into (Name of Organization), a (State) nonprofit corporation, pursuant to Section _____ of the (State) Nonprofit Corporation Act (the "Act"), does hereby make these Articles of Merger:

Article 1

Attached as <u>Exhibit A</u> is a copy of the Plan of Merger between _____ and _____ pursuant to which _____ will be merged with and into _____.

Article 2

The Plan of Merger has been adopted by the board of directors of _____ in accordance with the (State) Nonprofit

Corporation Code, as provided in Section _____ of the Act. On _____, 2000, at a meeting of the board of directors of _____, the Plan was adopted by the vote of a majority of the directors in office of _____.

Article 3

With respect to _____ there are _____ memberships of _____ outstanding all of which are of the same class. Each member is entitled to cast one vote. There were _____ members indisputably voting on the Plan of Merger. The number of votes cast FOR the Plan of Merger was _____, and the number of votes cast AGAINST the Plan of Merger was _____; and the number of votes cast FOR the Plan of Merger by the members of _____ was sufficient for approval by the members in accordance with the (State) Nonprofit Corporation Code, as provided in Section _____ of the Code.

Article 4

The merger shall be effective the ___ day of ___, 2000.

Sample Human Resource Resolutions

TAX DEFERRED ANNUITY PLAN OF THE
(NAME OF ORGANIZATION)
and
PARTICIPATING ASSOCIATED EMPLOYERS

AGREEMENT, made this _____ day of _____, 2000 by and between the (Name of Organization) and the (Name of Organization), EIN: _____, whose headquarters are located at the following address: _____.

WHEREAS, the (Organization) has established a Tax Deferred Annuity Plan ("Plan") for the benefit of its employees and which is known as the Tax Deferred Annuity Plan of the (Name of Organization) and Participating Associated Employers;

NOW, THEREFORE, the undersigned Corporation hereby adopts the Tax Deferred Annuity Plan to be effective as of (Date); and

FURTHER PROVIDED, the Board of Directors of the Corporation has authorized the Corporation's participation in the Plan;

NOW, THEREFORE, the (Organization) and the Corporation agree as follows:

1. Except as otherwise indicated, terms used herein have the same meaning they have under the Plan.

2. The Corporation shall participate in the Plan pursuant to the terms of the Plan.

3. For so long as the Corporation participates in the Plan, the Corporation agrees to make contributions according to the terms of the individual employee salary reduction agreements and the Internal Revenue Code.

4. The Board of Directors of the (Organization) may terminate this Agreement by giving thirty (30) days prior written notice to the Corporation.

5. The Corporation may terminate this Agreement and withdraw from the Plan at the end of any Plan year by giving thirty (30) days prior written notice to the Board, the Committee and the Annuity Providers. Upon such a termination, the rights of the Corporation, the Participants and Beneficiaries will be determined according to the terms of the Plan as then in effect and the Corporation, and the Participants and Beneficiaries shall not be entitled to withdraw or transfer any of the assets held by the Annuity Providers under the Plan except as permitted under the Plan and the Annuity Contracts.

IN WITNESS WHEREOF, the parties hereto have executed this Agreement as to the day and year first above written.

Attest: (Name of Corporation)

_____   By: _____
                                      Title: _____

Attest: (Name of Organization)

_____   By: _____
                                      Title: _____

ADOPTION AGREEMENT

FLEXIBLE BENEFIT PLAN OF THE (NAME OF ORGANIZATION)
&
PARTICIPATING AFFILIATED EMPLOYERS

AGREEMENT, made this _____ day of ____, 2000 by and between the (Name of Organization) and the (Name of Corporation), EIN: _____, whose headquarters are located at the following address: _____.

WHEREAS, the Society has established a Flexible Benefit Plan with certain contributions being made under Section (List section) of the Internal Revue Code for the benefit of its employees and which is known as the Flexible Benefits Program;

NOW, THEREFORE, the Board of Directors of the Corporation hereby adopts the Flexible Benefit Program effective as of (date) on behalf of its eligible employees as follows:

1. Eligible employees will be defined as: Full Time Employee's Standard Hours 37.5, Part Time Employee's Standard Hours 20. (Use corporate parameters.)
2. The Division will offer to its eligible employees all of the Benefit Plans or Policies with the exception of: (List exceptions.)
    a. Short Term Disability Plan
        Will be offered   Will not be offered
    b. Vision Service Plan
        Will be offered   Will not be offered
    c. Indemnity Medical Plan
        Will be offered   Will not be offered

NOW, THEREFORE, the (Name of Organization) and the Corporation agree as follows:

1. Except as otherwise indicated, terms used herein have the same meaning they have under the Plan.

2. The Corporation shall participate in the Plan pursuant to the provisions of the Plan.
3. For so long as the Corporation participates in the Plan, the Corporation agrees to reimburse the (Organization) for premiums paid on behalf of the Corporation's participants.
4. The National Home Office Board of Directors may terminate this Agreement at any time with thirty (30) days notice to the Corporation.
5. The Corporation may terminate this Agreement and withdraw from the Plan at the end of any Plan Year by giving notification to cancel participation prior to (End of fiscal year) of any given year to the Board, the Committee and the National Vice President of Human Resources. Upon such termination, the rights of the Corporation, the Participants and Beneficiaries will be determined according to the terms of the Plan as then in effect and the Corporation, and the Participants and Beneficiaries shall not be entitled to any other benefits under the Plan.
6. The Corporation further agrees to adhere to all underwriting guidelines as approved by the Board and attached hereto as Exhibit A and made a part hereof.

IN WITNESS WHEREOF, the parties hereto have executed this Agreement as to the day and year first above written.

Attest: (Name of Corporation)

_____   By: _____
                                            Title: _____

Attest: (Name of Organization)

_____   By: _____
                                            Title: _____

PARTICIPATION AGREEMENT

RETIREMENT ANNUITY PLAN
OF THE
(NAME OF ORGANIZATION)
AND
PARTICIPATING ASSOCIATED EMPLOYERS

AGREEMENT, made this ＿＿＿ day of ＿＿＿, 2000 by and between the (Name of Organization) and the (Name of Corporation).

WHEREAS, the (Name of Organization) has established a retirement annuity plan ("Plan") for the benefit of its employees and which is known as the Retirement Annuity Plan of the (Name of Organization) and Participating Associated Employers; and

WHEREAS, the Board of Directors of the Corporation has authorized the Corporation's participation in the Plan;

NOW, THEREFORE, the (Name of Organization) and the Corporation agree as follows:

1. Except as otherwise indicated, terms used herein have the same meaning they have for purposes of the Plan.

2. The Corporation shall participate in the Plan pursuant to Article (List article number) of the Plan and shall comply with all relevant provisions of the Plan.

3. For so long as the Corporation participates in the Plan, the Corporation agrees to make contributions as certified to it pursuant to the Plan.

4. The Corporation may terminate this Agreement and withdraw from the Plan at the end of any Plan Year by giving thirty (30) days' prior written notice of such intention to the Board, the Committee, and the Funding Agent. Upon such a termination the rights of the Corporation, the Par-

ticipants and Beneficiaries will be determined according to the terms of the Plan as then in effect and the Corporation, and the Participants and Beneficiaries shall not be entitled to withdraw or transfer any of the assets held by the Funding Agent under the Plan except as permitted under the terms of the Plan.

IN WITNESS WHEREOF, the parties hereto have executed this Agreement as to the day and year first above written.

(Name of Corporation)

Attest:

_____   By: _____
                                    Title: _____

Attest: (Name of Organization)

_____   By: _____
                                    Title: _____

RESOLUTION:

The (Name of Corporation) resolves to enter into agreements with the (Name of Organization) that permits participation in the Flexible Benefit Plan, the Tax Deferred Annuity Plan and the Retirement Annuity Plan and hereby orders the filing of all appropriate participation agreements.

Sample Banking Resolutions

CORPORATE RESOLUTION

TO WHOM IT MAY CONCERN:

I hereby certify that at a meeting of the Board of Directors of the (Name of Corporation), hereafter referred to as "this Corporation," a nonprofit Corporation organized and existing under and by virtue of the laws of the State of _____, held this __ day of _____ 20___ at which meeting a quorum was present and acting throughout, the following resolutions were adopted and ever since have been and now are in full force and effect as of the date thereof:

RESOLVED: That any two of the signatures of the following officers—Chairman of the Board, President, Chief Executive Officer (CEO), Treasurer, or the CEO's designee—of this Corporation shall be sufficient to make valid checks, vouchers, or checking accounts of this Corporation, provided, however, that in the case of a single check required either for any operating expense of less than ten thousand dollars ($10,000), or for any payroll of less than twenty five thousand dollars ($25,000), the signature of one of the above officers or other authorized person designated by the CEO shall be sufficient;

RESOLVED FURTHER: That, upon the recommendation of the Corporation Treasurer, any one of the signatures of the officers of this Corporation shall be sufficient for the deposit or withdrawal of funds to and from the following types of investment instruments:

1. U.S. Treasury and Government Agency Securities backed by the full faith and credit of the United States Government with maturities not to exceed 63 months.

2. Money market funds which invest in U.S. government and U.S. Government-insured agencies' securities only.

3. Regular savings accounts, time deposits, certificates of deposit in banks which are F.D.I.C. insured. The investment must not exceed $100,000 per institution, including aggregated accrued interest, unless the bank is rated A+ of A by the Sheshunoff Bank Quarterly Ranking Bank Service. In no event shall the total of balances in excess of $100,000 with one bank exceed the lower of 10% of investible assets or 10% of the bank's capital and surplus.

4. Combined Investment Pools. These pools shall be managed by professional investment advisors, and securities shall be held by an independent custodian.

RESOLVED FURTHER: That this Corporation may sell, at the appropriate time with appropriate Board input as determined by the Treasurer, all real property, and any other item donated to or received by this Corporation by legacy or otherwise, to be used by this Corporation without restriction;

RESOLVED FURTHER: That any one of the Chairman of the Board, Treasurer, CEO or the CEO's designee is empowered to execute and deliver any document or make any assignment and transfer necessary to complete such sales transactions, except as set forth herein;

RESOLVED FURTHER: That the Chairman of the Board, Treasurer, CEO or the CEO's designee is empowered to execute and deliver any document or make any assignment and transfer necessary to carry on the day-to-day business of this Corporation, except as set forth herein;

RESOLVED FURTHER: That the Chairman of the Board, Treasurer, CEO or the CEO's designee is empowered to transfer funds between and among savings accounts and checking accounts of this Corporation by written or telephonic instructions to the bank or other financial institution involved;

RESOLVED FURTHER: That the Corporation Resolution adopted at the Board of Directors meeting held on _____ is hereby revoked;

RESOLVED FURTHER: That the above resolutions shall remain in full force and effect until altered, amended or revoked by the Board of Directors of this Corporation.

I further certify that the authority hereby conferred is not inconsistent with the Charter or Bylaws of this Corporation, and a true and correct list of the officers of this Corporation, as of the present date, is listed below and will be printed on the letterhead:

CHAIRMAN, BOARD OF DIRECTORS
VICE CHAIRMAN, BOARD OF DIRECTORS
SECRETARY, BOARD OF DIRECTORS
TREASURER, BOARD OF DIRECTORS
CHIEF EXECUTIVE OFFICER

> In witness, whereof, I have hereunto set my hand and the Seal of this Corporation, this _____ day of _____, _____.
>
> _____
> (name of signer)

List of Documents Frequently Required in Merger

- Plan and Agreement to Merge

- Notice of meetings in which merger is discussed

- Notice of meeting at which merger is voted upon

- Any waiver of proper notice signed by appropriate parties

- Evidence of Plan and Agreement to Merge being mailed within proper notice time frames

- Notice of bylaws modifications (unless covered in the Plan and Agreement to Merge)

- Notice of Articles of Incorporation modification (unless covered in the Plan and Agreement to Merge)

- Evidence of bylaws modifications (if required)

- Evidence of Articles of Incorporation modifications (if required)

- Certificate of Authority to do Business (in all states/regions)

- Renewal of License to Solicit Funds (where required)

- Registration as a public charity (where required)

- Minutes of all meetings at which merger-related votes were taken

- Notice of court hearings to dissenting votes where required

- Notice in newspaper of public record where required

- All other pertinent ancillary documents

Sample Certificates of Authority To Do Business

SECRETARY OF STATE

CERTIFICATE OF DOCUMENT FILED

The Secretary of State acknowledge receipt of the following document.

Application for Certificate of Authority

The document was filed on August 31, 1998, at 9:05 AM, to be effective as of August 31, 1998, at 9:05 AM.

The amount of $25.00 was received in full payment of the filing fee.

_____

SECRETARY OF STATE

SECRETARY OF STATE

CERTIFICATE OF GOOD STANDING

I, _____, Secretary of State of _____, do certify that: The corporation listed below is a corporation formed under the laws of _____, that the corporation was formed by the filing of Articles of Incorporation with the Office of the Secretary of State on the date listed below: that the corporation is governed by the Chapter of _____ Statutes listed below, and that this corporation is authorized to do business as a corporation at the time this certificate is issued.

NAME:

DATE FORMED:

CHAPTER GOVERNED BY:

This certificate has been issued on August 26, 1998

_____
SECRETARY OF STATE

SECRETARY OF STATE	APPLICATION FOR CERTIFICATE OF AUTHORITY (Nonprofit)

TO THE SECRETARY OF STATE_____:

Pursuant to the _____Nonprofit Corporation Act, the undersigned corporation applies for a certificate of authority to transact business in ____, and states:

1. The name of the corporation is _____

2. The corporation is incorporated under the laws of the state of _____

3. The date of incorporation of the corporation was   _____

4. The duration of the corporation is _____

5. The street address of its principal office is
    Address_____
    City, zip _____

6. The street address of its registered office in _____ and the name of its registered agent at that office
    Name   _____
    Address_____
    City, state, zip _____

7. The names and business addresses of its current directors and officers
    Name   _____
    Address_____
    City, state, zip _____

    Name   _____
    Address_____
    City, state, zip _____

    Name   _____
    Address_____
    City, state, zip _____
    Name   _____

Address _____

City, state, zip _____

Name   _____

Address _____

City, state, zip _____

(Please attach additional pages as necessary)

  8. A brief description of the purposes the corporation will pursue in ___

     _____

     _____

  9. A certificate of existence, or a document of similar import, duly authenticated by the official having custody of corporate records in the state or country of incorporation, accompanies this application.

10. I certify under penalty of perjury and pursuant to the laws of the State of _____ that the preceding is true and correct.

     Date _____

     President or Vice-President _____

     Secretary or Assistant Secretary _____

NOTES:

1. The filing fee is $25.00. Make checks payable to SECRETARY OF STATE.

2. Two signatures are required. The document is to be signed by the president or vice-president of the corporation, and by the secretary or assistant secretary.

SECRETARY OF STATE

Corporations Division

APPENDIX **K**

Sample Meeting Notes

XYZ Corporation
Board of Directors Meeting
January 17, 1999

The XYZ Corporation held a Board of Directors meeting at 10:00 am on January 17, 1999 at the corporate offices. Twenty-six members were present. The secretary recognized the meeting as official with a quorum present in person.

The introduction was given by the Chairman of the Board of Directors, followed by a welcome given by the President.

There was an overview of the history of the strategic alliance between Corporation and the proposed merger partners presented.

Next was a report on the potential relationship between the Corporation and the proposed merger partners including the aspects of how such a new merged organization will function.

Following was review of the documents outlining the formal relationship between the above noted parties. It was noted that the resolution on which the Board is contemplating contains all the points in the Plan and Agreement to merge, by reference, that was sent to the Board with proper notice and is incorporated within the scope of the resolution. Following was a review regarding the points of the Agreement.

There was a review of the changes contemplated, by the Plan and Agreement to Merge, for the bylaws and Certificate of Incorporation and indicated that proper notice of the proposed changes was mailed, by registered mail, to the members of the Board of Directors.

Next, followed discussions, comments, questions and answers.

A motion was made by (Name) to approve the resolution as presented. The Motion was seconded by (Name).

The Motion passed unanimously.

The meeting was adjourned at 12:00 noon.

Respectfully submitted,

Secretary

APPENDIX L

Strategic Restructuring:

Findings from a Study of Integrations and Alliances Among Nonprofit Social Service and Cultural Organizations in the United States

A FTER THE TEXT OF THIS BOOK was typeset and prior to publication, an important piece of research in the nonprofit merger field was published by the Chapin Hall Center for Children at the University of Chicago. The work, entitled *"Strategic Restructuring: Findings from a Study of Integrations and Alliances Among Nonprofit Social Service and Cultural Organizations in the United States"* by Amelia Kohm, David La Piana and Heather Gowdy, June 2000, contains information that is important and valuable to any reader considering nonprofit merger and alliances.

Earlier work of La Piana is quoted throughout the text of this book. An executive summary with excerpts of the report is included with permission in this appendix. The report may be purchased from the Chapin Hall Center for Children at the University of Chicago (773) 256-5100 or on their website at www.chapin.uchicago.edu.

The Chapin Hall Center for Children, a policy research center at the University of Chicago, and Strategic Solutions, a California-based project of the consulting firm La Piana Associates, Inc., surveyed 192 nonprofit social services and cultural organizations in the United States that had experience with strategic restructuring. Drawing on descriptive data provided by respondents, they devised a typology that includes two primary types:

Alliance. An alliance is a strategic restructuring that includes a commitment to continue for the foreseeable future, shared or transferred decision-making power, and some type of formal agreement. However, it does not involve any change to the corporate structure of the participating organizations.

Integration. An integration is a strategic restructuring that includes changes to corporate control and/or structure, including the creation or dissolution of one or more organizations.

Key findings from the analysis of survey responses include the following:

- Organizations involved in integrations were more likely than organizations involved in alliances to be focused on human services, to have large budgets, to have active boards, and to be located in urban communities.

- Organizations involved in alliances were more likely than organizations involved in integrations to be focused on arts and culture, to have small budgets, to have fairly inactive boards of directors, and to be located in rural communities.

- Integrations usually involved fewer organizations than alliances did.

- Very young and old organizations were less likely to be involved in any type of strategic restructuring.

- Competition is a key factor in strategic restructuring. It appears that certain industries or service areas are growing crowded with nonprofits and, in some cases, for-profits and governmental organizations. Organizations are attempting to temper competition by cooperating or merging.

- Respondents entered into a strategic restructuring more often to improve the quality or range of what they do and the efficiency with which they do it than because of any immediate threats of closure or pressure from funders. In other words, they appear to be

approaching strategic restructuring as a result of forecasting and planning.

- The most common benefits that respondents reported from their restructuring experiences were: increased programmatic collaborations with partner organizations, increased services, increased administrative capacity/quality, and increased market share.

- Respondents generally reported very positive strategic restructuring experiences without significant problems. Most felt that they realized their goals for the partnership. Additionally, in assessing a list of thirteen potential problems, no more than 36% of survey respondents identified any individual problem as significant or very significant.[1]

- The most common challenges, according to respondents, were: conflicting organizational cultures, the adjustment of staff to new roles/positions, building trust among organizations, and autonomy concerns. Integrations presented more challenges to respondent organizations than did alliances.

- The most important success factors, according to respondents, were: a staff or board member who championed the partnership, positive past experiences with partnering with other organizations, board support encouragement, and organizational risk taking or growth orientation.

It is important to note the characteristics of the organizations surveyed.

1. There was a mix of organizations, although 73% described themselves as being engaged in human services while 18% said they were arts and cultural organizations, 9% described themselves as "other."

---

[1]Because the sample was entirely self-selected, it is likely that it represents more successful strategic restructuring experiences than unsuccessful ones because those who have experienced great difficulties or failures may be less likely to participate in these types of surveys.

2. Forty-six percent of the organizations ranged in age of existence from 11 years to 60. 21% had been in existence for 10 years or less and 33% had been in operation for more than 60 years.

3. The budget size of the organizations were as follows:

Less than $100,000	3%
$100,000 - $500,00	17%
$500,000 - $1 million	10%
$1 million - $5 million	36%
$5 million - $10 million	18%
more than $10 million	16%

4. The organizations described their location as:

9%	Rural
23%	Suburban
50%	Urban
19%	More than one type of community

5. The type of restructuring among the organizations were:

Alliances	45%
Administrative Consolidation	(35%)
Joint Programming	(10%)
Integrations	55%
Management Service Organization	(18%)
Joint Venture	(2%)
Parent/Sub	(3 %)
Merger	(32%)

6. Eighty-one percent of all respondents indicated they had entered into the relationship within the last five years.

The report drew an interesting conclusion worthy of including in this summary regarding the factors that initiated the restructuring within their organizations. These factors are:

- A sudden interruption in the status quo—such as the departure of a director, a fiscal crisis, or a significant funding opportunity—that requires or propels an organization to make a significant change.

- Forward-thinking individuals (usually executive directors) who shepherd a strategic restructuring idea through opposition, some-

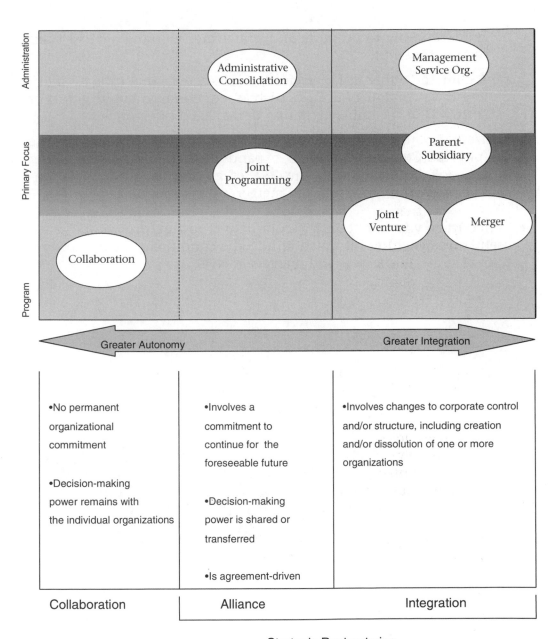

Figure L–1 The Partnership Matrix

times working to promote and sometimes working against their own self-interest.

- A climate—either real, perceived, or predicted—that calls for a different way of doing business, such as reductions in public grants or contracts or the implementation of managed care policies.

Figure L–1, shown above, developed by Strategic Solutions and the Chapin Hall Center for Children, expands on a chart presented earlier in the book, but includes a more detailed graphic look at the relationship between autonomy and full merger integration.

I encourage you to obtain the complete report excerpted above for useful and insightful information into the conditions, factors, and results of strategic alliances and mergers in NPOs.

Index